Culinary Creations

from Sonoma Wine Country
Volume 2

WINE COUNTRY
BED AND BREAKFAST
GRACIOUS **INNS** SERVICE
OF SONOMA COUNTY

Favorite Recipes
from Bed & Breakfast Inns, Wineries, and Other Purveyors

Culinary Creations from Sonoma Wine Country
Volume 2
Favorite Recipes from Bed & Breakfast Inns, Wineries, and Other Purveyors

Published by:
Wine Country Inns of Sonoma County
P.O. Box 51B
Geyserville, CA 95441
1-800-946-3268

Wine Country Inns is grateful to all the photo contributors to this cookbook.
Front cover photo courtesy of Christine Gustafson, www.innlightmarketing.com
Back cover photo courtesy of Jeff Wilber
Designer/Production Editor: Susan Degive, www.degivellc.com

Printing History:
     June 2010   First Edition
Printed in China

ISBN: 0-9769797-1-5

Table Of Contents

Signature Recipe: **Belgian Endive and Apple Salad with Blue Cheese Dressing and Walnuts**

Signature Recipe: **Crustless Quiche Lorraine**
Baileys Inspired Chocolate Fondue
Beignets
Bellini
Brioche Pain Perdu
Pear Ginger Crepes
Tarte Tartin

Signature Recipe: **Mexican Soufflé**
Baked Pears
Banana Nut Pancakes with Spiced Syrup
Double Corn Muffins
Eggs Benedict
Quick Drop Biscuits
Lemon Blueberry Scones

Signature Recipe: **Birmingham Eggs**
Baked Apples
Broiled Blueberries
Chili Cheese Puff
Italian Easter Pie
Peach Soup
Stuffed Tomatoes

Signature Recipe: **Apple Ham Breakfast Bread Pudding**
Baked Brie and Tomato Breakfast Strata
Citrus Mini Cakes
Farmer's Breakfast
Lemon Chiffon Smoothie
Muffins That Taste Like Donuts
Rich Chocolate Bundt Cake

Culinary Creations from Sonoma Wine Country

Culinary Creations from Sonoma Wine Country

Table of Contents

Culinary Creations from Sonoma Wine Country

Introduction

Dear Reader,

Sonoma Wine Country has become a destination not only for those in search of world-class wine, but also for outstanding cuisine. Visitors, locals and food critics use words such as "fresh," "innovative" and "distinctive" to describe the culinary delights available in Sonoma.

Because guests so often ask for our recipes, Wine Country Inns of Sonoma County is proud to offer this cookbook: a compilation of recipes from member inns as well as a select group of wineries and other purveyors in the county. You'll find a sampling of culinary favorites to make at home and to share with family and friends.

We hope you'll visit the inns, wineries, and other establishments you'll read about in the following pages. When you do, you're likely to taste some of the delicious recipes in this cookbook and the award-winning cuisine of Sonoma Wine Country.

Bon appétit,

Wine Country Inns of Sonoma County
www.WineCountryInns.com

P.S. We have taken great care with testing and editing these recipes to eliminate any errors in content or procedure. However, we may have missed something and invite you to share with us any mistakes, points of confusion, or omissions so that we can correct the recipes for future publications.

To order additional books, contact us on the Website above, by email, or by telephone.

*Contact us by email at
info@winecountryinns.com
or by telephone at
1.800.946.3268.*

About Wine Country Inns of Sonoma County

Wine Country Inns is an association of select bed and breakfast inns located throughout the many renowned wine regions in Sonoma County California. All members adhere to the highest standards of excellence in accommodations, amenities, cuisine, and hospitality.

Bed and breakfast inns provide a unique experience for guests. As small inns, we offer personal attention and can customize your visit to match your needs and expectations. Whether you are looking for a secluded getaway high on a hillside, historic home in town, or cottage with a view of vineyards, we have an inn that will suit you.

"Assured Elegance On Wine Country Accommodations"

For more information about member inns, including availability, visit us on the Web at:

www.WineCountryInns.com
or call us at:
1-800-WINECOUNTRY (946-3268)

About Wine Country Inns

WCI INNS:

Applewood Inn
www.applewoodinn.com

Auberge on the Vineyard
www.aubergeonthevineyard.com

Avalon, a Luxury Bed & Breakfast
www.avalonluxuryinn.com

Birmingham Bed & Breakfast
www.birminghambb.com

Camellia Inn
www.camelliainn.com

Case Ranch Inn
www.caseranchinn.com

English Tea Garden Inn
www.teagardeninn.com

Glenelly Inn & Cottages
www.glenelly.com

Hidden Oak Inn
www.hiddenoakinn.com

Hope-Merrill Bed & Breakfast Inn
www.hope-inns.com

Inn at Occidental
www.innatoccidental.com

Irish Rose Inn
www.theirishroseinn.com

Melitta Station Inn
www.melittastationinn.com

Old Crocker Inn
www.oldcrockerinn.com

Santa Nella House Bed and Breakfast
www.santanellahouse.com

The Gables Wine Country Inn
www.thegablesinn.com

The Raford Inn
www.rafordinn.com

Vintage Towers Bed & Breakfast Inn
www.vintagetowers.com

Exploring Sonoma County

New arrivals to Sonoma County are taken aback by the spectacular beauty. The county has a remarkable variety of scenery – from the rugged splendor of the Pacific coast, along coastal hills with rambling ranches and the remnants of apple and citrus orchards, to Jack London's beloved inland mountains. And ranging over all is the breathtaking symmetry of the vineyards.

Over 50 miles of coastline extend from Bodega Bay in the south to Gualala in the north. Follow migrating whales, gaze at seal pups basking in the sunshine, spot oystercatchers dipping for their dinner, or enjoy barbequed local oyster delicacies at a seaside restaurant.

Numerous parks populate the county where the walker, nature lover and bird watcher can roam through redwoods, along trails and creeks, around Lake Sonoma, and above the Valley of the Moon. Opportunities abound along the Russian River for rafting, kayaking, canoeing and swimming as it winds its way to the Pacific Ocean. Bike riders relish both the challenge of the hills and miles of easy pedaling. Or invigorate yourself with a horseback ride in the redwoods or along the beach.

And when you have had enough activity, sit awhile on the banks of the Russian River. Picture the early Russian settlers after whom the river is named, as they hunted for the valuable skins of animals such as mink and beaver that once roamed in abundance. Upstream is the unique Santa Rosa Laguna,

seasonal wetlands for migrating birds.

Sonoma weather is ideal for grapes with 11 wine appellations taking advantage of microclimates that range from the heat of the Dry Creek and Alexander Valleys to the cooler appellations of the Sonoma Coast and Russian River. Luther Burbank, the famed horticulturalist, settled in Sonoma County

Exploring Sonoma County

and developed new strains of fruits, vegetables and flowers such as the Santa Rosa plum and the Shasta daisy.

In the 2009 Gallup-Healthways Well-Being Index, based on interviews with 353,000 Americans, people in Sonoma were found to be happier and healthier than anywhere else in California. The county ranked fifth overall in the nation.

Experience the county's well-being in its small towns, rich with history and appeal:

- Cloverdale: A quiet getaway town at the north end of the Alexander Valley near Lake Sonoma, centrally located for visits to Napa, Mendocino, and Sonoma counties.

- Forestville: A relaxing spot near the Russian River in the Green Valley appellation.

- Geyserville: A quaint convenient hamlet at the heart of the Alexander Valley.

- Glen Ellen: A romantic Valley of the Moon locale near Jack London State Park.

- Guerneville: A small tourist town situated between the Russian River and surrounding hills, home of Armstrong Redwood State Park.

- Healdsburg: Shopping, restaurants, and wine tasting around the downtown plaza, easy access to the Russian River, Dry Creek and Alexander Valley wineries.

- Kenwood: In the Valley of the Moon amid vineyards, walnut orchards and groves of oak trees.

- Occidental: A charming township on the Bohemian Highway, a scenic drive through towering redwoods, green pastures and rocky ravines.

- Santa Rosa: The county seat with numerous restaurants, central to all Sonoma county and Napa Valley wineries, most of which lie less than 30 minutes away.

- Sebastopol: Small semi-urban community known for Gravenstein apples, antiquing, canoeing and hiking.

- Sonoma: The original capital of the "Bear Flag Republic" with central plaza, historic mission complex and shopping and dining.

Sonoma County boasts abundant fresh produce, cheese producers, olive groves, artisan bakeries, organic coffee-roasters, free-range poultry and livestock. These many ingredients – increasingly organic and bio-dynamic – are woven into dining magic at scores of restaurants, some grand and renowned, others intimate and often locally-kept secrets. Whatever your delight you can find it in our beautiful and bounteous county.

When to Visit:

Sonoma County is a year-round destination with warm, breezy summers and mild, green winters. Wineries are open all year. Listed below are some of the appealing events in the area (visit www.sonoma.com for details and more events).

JANUARY
• Winter Wineland, Russian River Wine Road • Whale Watching along the Sonoma Coast
• Old Time Fiddle Contest & Festival, Cloverdale • Sonoma Valley Olive Festival

FEBRUARY
• Citrus Fair, Cloverdale • Romancing the Vine, Santa Rosa • VinOlivo, Sonoma • Valentine Chocolate Pairing at Wineries • Healdsburg Wild Steelhead Festival • Sonoma Valley Olive Festival
• Crab Feeds • Sonoma Crab & Wine Festival

MARCH
• Barrel Tasting, Russian River Wine Road & Sonoma Valley Wine Country • Home and Garden Show, Santa Rosa • Cycling Classic, Santa Rosa

APRIL
• Whale Watching • Fisherman's Festival, Bodega Bay • April in Carneros, Sonoma • Apple Blossom Festival, Sebastopol • Passport to Dry Creek Valley • Historic Homes Walking Tour, Healdsburg • Sonoma International Film Festival • Farmers Markets

MAY
• Luther Burbank Rose Parade, Santa Rosa • Western Days, Cloverdale • California Outdoor Sports Championships, Infineon Raceway • Sonoma Jazz Plus Music Festival • Memorial Weekend Antique Faire, Healdsburg • Country Fair and Twilight Parade, Healdsburg • Passport to Sonoma Valley • AMGEN Tour of California • Vintage Race Car Festival & Races, Sonoma • AMA Super Bike Showdown, Infineon Raceway • Farmers Markets

JUNE
• Sonoma Marin Fair, Petaluma • Lavender Festivals: Healdsburg, Kenwood, Santa Rosa • Toyota/Save Mart 350 NASCAR, Infineon Raceway • Art at the Source Open Studio , western Sonoma County • Taste of the Valley, Alexander Valley Wine Growers • Tuesday Summer Concert Series, Healdsburg • Ox Roast, Sonoma Plaza • Healdsburg Jazz Festival • Farmers Markets

JULY
• Old Fashioned Fourth of July Fireworks, Sonoma, Healdsburg, Cloverdale, Santa Rosa • Hot Air Balloon Classic • Annual Showcase: Taste of Sonoma Wine and Food • FRAM Autolite NHRA Nationals, Infineon Raceway • Dixieland Jazz Festival, Sonoma • Wine Country Half Marathon, Sonoma • Vineman Ironman 70.3, Santa Rosa • Sonoma County Fair • Antique Fair and Harvest Century Bicycle Tour, Healdsburg • Tuesday Summer Concert Series, Healdsburg • Farmers Markets

AUGUST
• Accordion Festival, Cotati • Sonoma County Fair • Santa Rosa Marathon • Grape to Glass, Russian River Valley • Wine Country Film Festival, Sonoma • Guitar Festival, Tuesday Summer Concert Series, Healdsburg • Friday Night Live Concert Series, Cloverdale • Farmers Markets
• Grand Prix of Sonoma Country Indy Car Series, Infineon Raceway

SEPTEMBER
• Russian River Jazz Festival, Guerneville • Sonoma Valley Harvest Wine Auction • Labor Day Weekend Antique Fair, Healdsburg • Street Celebration-Antique Car Show, Cloverdale • Beer on the Plaza, Healdsburg • Valley of the Moon Vintage Festival, Sonoma • Farmers Markets

OCTOBER
• Charles Schwab Cup Championship, Sonoma • Levi's GRAND DONDO Cycling Tour • Harvest Fair, Santa Rosa • ARTrails Open Studio Tour • Oktoberfest Celebrations • Pumpkin Festival, Healdsburg
• Fall Colors Festival & Vintage Car Show, Geyserville • Pinot on the River, Russian River Valley •
Farmers Markets

NOVEMBER
• Wine and Food Affair, Russian River Wine Road • Santa's Riverboat Arrival, Petaluma • Victorian Holiday Celebration, Petaluma • Holiday in Carneros, Sonoma • Heart of Sonoma Valley Holiday Open House

DECEMBER
• Heritage Homes Parlor Tour, Petaluma • Victorian House Tour, Healdsburg • Holiday Open Houses, Teas and Festivities • Black & White Ball, Geyserville • Sonoma Valley Olive Festival
• Cornerstone Lighting of the Snowmen, Sonoma

"Reignite your passion... live an indelible experience in this romantic Sonoma Wine Country Getaway"

Surrounded by world-class wineries, a short walk from the Russian river and Armstrong Redwood Park and a spectacular short drive away from the stunning Sonoma coast, Applewood Inn, Restaurant and Spa is located near Guerneville, in the western Russian River valley.

This luxury Bed and Breakfast is an historical mansion nested among towering redwoods, serene gardens and fruit trees. Its 19 rooms and acclaimed restaurant offer refined and generous hospitality and evoke the warm welcome of a Tuscan villa.

Applewood Inn, Restaurant & Spa
www.applewoodinn.com
707-869-9093 • 800-555-8509
13555 Highway 116 • Guerneville, CA 95446

Signature Recipe

Belgian Endive and Apple Salad With Blue Cheese Dressing and Walnuts

4 apples, peeled
1 cup walnut halves, toasted in oven at 350 degrees Fahrenheit for 8 minutes
7 Belgian endives
1 cup blue cheese, crumbled
1/4 cup toasted walnut oil
1/2 cup chives, chopped
1/2 cup Blue Cheese Dressing

Cut apples into 1-inch cubes and sprinkle with a little lemon juice. Cut the endives crosswise into 1-inch slices. Keep the cores; they are the best part. Toss the endives apples with half the crumbled blue cheese, walnuts, chives and another drizzle of walnut oil.

Blue Cheese Dressing

1 cup mayonnaise
1 cup sour cream
8 ounces blue cheese, crumbled
1 shallot, finely diced and soaked in 1 tablespoon sherry vinegar
2 teaspoons garlic, finely chopped
2 good shots of Tabasco sauce
2 good shots of Worcestershire sauce
Salt and pepper to taste
Juice of 1/2 lemon
1/4 cup of buttermilk

This dressing is as easy to make as putting all the ingredients into a bowl and whisking vigorously until they are well combined. If too thick add buttermilk. Seasoning can be adjusted to taste with salt, pepper, lemon juice or Tabasco.

Serves: 4

Nestled in a lush vineyard between Healdsburg and the beautiful Mendocino Coast, Auberge on the Vineyard is a turn of the century bed and breakfast inn which combines luxurious Queen Anne architecture with a distinctive French twist. Guests may savor a delightful French-inspired breakfast, which undoubtedly tastes better when served with a large helping of the enchanting Alexander Valley vineyard views offered along the wraparound verandah.

Auberge on the Vineyard

www.aubergeonthevineyard.com
707-894-5956 • 800-833-6479
29955 River Road • Cloverdale, CA 95425

Signature Recipe

Crustless Quiche Lorraine

This is a very easy recipe that has been served for family and friends since I was a small child. In fact, even a child can prepare it (as long as they are old enough to read), and are sensible enough to use hot mitts when they remove the dish from the oven.

- 5 slices of thick bacon
- 1/2 medium size onion
- 2 tablespoons butter
- 8 ounces Gruyere
- 1 tablespoon flour
- 5 eggs
- 1 1/2 cups half and half
- Pinch each of white pepper and nutmeg

Preheat oven to 375 degrees Fahrenheit.

Cook the bacon, drain and crumble. Peel and slice the onion thinly. Melt butter in small skillet and cook onion until soft and translucent. Grate the cheese, mix in the flour, and set aside. Combine eggs, half and half, pepper and nutmeg and blend together at low speed until thoroughly mixed.

Grease a 10-inch round shallow pie pan. Layer crumbled bacon, onion, and cheese/flour mixture into pan. Pour egg mixture over top. Bake for 45 to 50 minutes, or until toothpick comes out clean.

Serves: 6

Bailey's Inspired Chocolate Fondue

8 ounces high quality dark chocolate, preferably 70% cocoa or higher
4 ounces Bailey's Irish Cream
4 ounces heavy cream
Assorted bite-sized or sliced fruits, such as apples, grapes, apricots,
bananas, strawberries, oranges

Prepare fruit and refrigerate.

Melt chocolate in double boiler. Simmer water (do not boil). Mix cream and Bailey's with the chocolate.

Serve in small fondue pot. Use fondue forks to spear fruits, dip in chocolate. Moaning is optional.

Serves: 6

Beignets

New Orleans is a decadent combination of interesting architecture, great blues, and outstanding food. It's where the beignet first attained fame. Rumor has it that beignets are a cousin to "pets de nonne," which translates roughly to "nun's farts". So remember, each time you take a bite out of these fabulous breakfast treats, you'll be providing a little "fuel" that will uplift a nun just a smidge closer to heaven.

  1 envelope active dry yeast
  1 1/2 cups warm water (approx. 105°)
  1/2 cup granulated sugar
  1 teaspoon salt
  1 teaspoon vanilla
  2 eggs, beaten
  1 cup milk
  7 cups all-purpose flour
  1/4 cup butter, softened
  Oil for deep-frying
  Powdered sugar

In large bowl, sprinkle yeast over the warm water; stir to dissolve and let stand for 5 minutes. Add sugar, salt, beaten eggs, and milk. Whisk or use electric mixer to blend thoroughly. Add 4 cups of the flour; beat until smooth. Add butter; gradually blend in remaining flour. Cover with plastic wrap and chill at least 4 hours or overnight.

In heavy pot heat about 2 inches of oil to 360 degrees Fahrenheit.

Roll out on floured board to 1/8-inch thickness. Cut into 2 1/2 to 3-inch squares. Deep fry for 2 to 3 minutes until lightly browned on both sides. Drain on paper towels and sprinkle generously with powdered sugar. Serve hot with French Press coffee.

Note: Dough can be cut and frozen. Using wax paper, be sure to separate the sqaures from each other when freezing.

Yield: 4 to 5 dozen.

Bellini

The Bellini was invented by Giuseppe Cipriani, in honor of the painter, Giovanni Bellini. First served at Harry's Bar in Venice, Italy, this cocktail and the fact that the place was a hang out for writer Ernest Hemingway put the bar on the international map of places to see and be seen. The Bellini is a sexy summer drink, best served up with fabulous friends, food, and in our little corner of the world, expansive vineyard views.

> 1/4 cup pureed peaches, or substitute Hiram Walker white peach schnapps
> 6 to 8 ounces dry champagne

Mix together and serve in champagne flutes.

Brioche Pain Perdu

I invented this truly decadent breakfast treat for leftover brioche which has impressed even the toughest critics, who, in my case, turned out to be the construction crew we flew in from the Midwest to remodel the inn. Apparently, these men felt that any food item which could not be pronounced in monosyllables was inedible. Needless to say, these men did not eat quiche. They did however, to a man, LOVE this dish!

A note of warning: Lest you be disappointed when this dish comes out of the oven, be prepared to be unimpressed by the look of it. It's not pretty, but boy, does it ever taste good.

Prep Time: 45 minutes, plus overnight refrigeration

> 4 to 6 stale brioche, depending upon their size, or substitute Challah bread
> 1/2 cup butter
> 1/4 cup brown sugar
> 3/4 cup cream
> 5 eggs
> 1 cup milk or half and half
> 1 teaspoon vanilla
> Pinch salt
> Cinnamon

In small saucepan, melt the butter, brown sugar and cream together. Bring to boil and cook at medium high heat for 2 to 3 minutes. Spread on bottom of buttered 13x9-inch glass pan.

Slice the brioche vertically into 3 to 4 pieces, approximately 1/4 inch in diameter.

Mix together the remaining ingredients. Dip the brioche in the egg mixture and arrange on top of brown sugar mixture. Pour remaining egg mixture over the top of the brioche, and sprinkle with cinnamon. Cover pan and refrigerate overnight to allow egg mixture to soak into the brioche.

Preheat oven to 350 degrees Fahrenheit.

Place a greased cookie sheet over the top of the glass pan with the brioche. Flip the brioche onto the cookie sheet and bake for about 20 to 25 minutes. Turn oven to broil and cook brioche for 3 to 4 minutes until the top is bubbly. Serve with syrup or just plain.

Yield: 24

Pear Ginger Crepes

  1 cup all-purpose flour
  1/2 cup milk
  1/2 cup water
  2 eggs
  2 tablespoons butter, melted
  1 teaspoon molasses
  1/2 teaspoon pure vanilla extract
  1/2 teaspoon cinnamon
  1/4 teaspoon dried ginger
  1/4 teaspoon salt
  1/8 teaspoon grated nutmeg

Whisk together all the ingredients and mix until smooth. Refrigerate and rest batter for 20 minutes.

Melt a little butter in a crepe pan over medium heat. Add 3 tablespoons of batter to the pan and swirl until the bottom of the pan is covered with batter. Cook the crepe for 1 minute, or until slightly moist on top and golden underneath. Loosen the edges of the crepe, slide spatula under and gently flip upside down into the pan. Cook for 1 minute and transfer the cooked crepe to a plate to keep warm.

Pear Topping

  Four pears, peeled and sliced
  4 tablespoons butter
  1/2 cup brown sugar
  1/2 teaspoon ground ginger

Melt butter and brown sugar in sauté pan. Gently add pears, and cook on medium low heat for about 7 to 8 minutes. Sprinkle with ginger.

To plate: Fold two crepes separately on plate. Lay pears on top. Serve warm.

Serves: 6

Auberge on the Vineyard

Tarte Tatin

Frozen puff pastry sheet (from a 17 1/4-ounce package)
1/2 stick (1/4 cup) unsalted butter, softened
1/2 cup sugar
6 to 8 Gala apples (about 3 pounds), peeled, cored and sliced approxi-
    mately 1/8 inch thick
1 teaspoon cinnamon
1/2 teaspoon each cloves and nutmeg
1/8 cup Calvados, cognac, or brandy

Preheat oven to 425 Fahrenheit.

Roll pastry sheet into a 10 1/2-inch square on a floured work surface with a floured rolling pin. Brush off excess flour and cut out a 10-inch round with a sharp knife, using a plate as guide. Transfer round to a baking sheet and chill.

Spread butter thickly on bottom and side of 10-inch heavy skillet and pour sugar evenly over bottom. Arrange as many apples as will fit vertically on sugar, packing them tightly in concentric circles. Apples will stick up above rim of skillet. Cook apples over moderate heat, undisturbed, until juices are deep golden and bubbling, approximately 20 minutes. Don't worry if juices color unevenly. Pour Calvados over the apples. Lay pastry round over apples.

Bake tart until pastry is browned, 20 to 25 minutes. Transfer skillet to a rack and cool at least 10 minutes.

Just before serving, invert a platter with lip over skillet and, using potholders to hold skillet and plate tightly together, invert tart into 10-inch pastry dish. Replace any apples that stick to skillet. Brush any excess caramel from skillet over apples. Serve immediately.

Serves: 8

Close your eyes and imagine an enchanted forest... A charming Tudor house is nestled amidst towering redwoods where aromatic afternoon tea and mouth-watering cookies await you on the deck or in the cozy den. Our exquisite B&B hosts your fantasy getaway with outrageous style and genuine hospitality. The unique decor transports you into a misty world of magic and fancy. A delectable, plentiful feast is served each morning in the elegant yet comfortable dining room where you will meet new friends at the breakfast table. Here anything is possible, so recharge your imagination. This is Avalon, your secret hideaway.

Avalon, a Luxury Bed & Breakfast
www.avalonluxuryinn.com
707-824-0880
11910 Graton Road • Sebastopol, CA 95472

Signature Recipe

Mexican Soufflé

6 large chiles, roasted (or use canned Ortega chiles)
1 1/2 cups Monterey Jack cheese, grated
1 1/2 cups medium sharp cheddar cheese, grated
12 eggs
1 cup milk
2 tablespoons all-purpose flour (may be omitted if cooking gluten-free)
1 teaspoon salt
1 small clove of fresh garlic, minced
1 teaspoon cilantro, minced fresh or dried
1 teaspoon oregano, minced fresh or dried
1 teaspoon cumin powder
1/2 teaspoon ground pepper

Preheat oven to 350 degrees Fahrenheit.

Grease a 9x11-inch baking dish. Coarsely chop chiles and layer on bottom of baking dish. Mix grated cheeses and sprinkle over chiles. Whirl remaining ingredients in a blender until well mixed. Pour over cheese. Bake 45 minutes. Let stand a few minutes before serving.

Serve with salsa, guacamole and sour cream.

Serves: 8

Baked Pears

3 large hard green pears
1/2 cup brown sugar
1 teaspoon ground cinnamon
1/2 teaspoon grated nutmeg
1 tablespoon butter
3 tablespoons orange juice
Vanilla bean ice cream

Preheat oven to 350 degrees Fahrenheit.

Cut pears in half lengthwise and remove the cores. Sprinkle brown sugar and spices on bottom of baking dish. Place the pear halves, cut side down, on top of the sugar and spices. Dot the pear backs with the butter and drizzle the orange juice over the sugar/spice mixture. Bake for approximately 1 hour, or until pears are tender. Pears that are riper will need less time in the oven. Serve cut side up with small scoop of vanilla bean ice cream.

Serves: 6

Banana Nut Pancakes with
Spiced Syrup

One of Avalon's most popular recipes started as Buttermilk Pancakes with organic maple syrup. To spice things up we added banana which was delicious but the maple syrup was not a good complement to the banana flavor. As they say, necessity is the mother of invention! When the hunt for a better match turned up nothing perfect, Hilary created Spiced Syrup, which complements the pancakes perfectly. The nuts were the last addition, adding a hearty crunch.

1 ripe banana, mashed
1 egg
1 1/4 cups buttermilk
2 tablespoons safflower oil
    (or any light oil)

1 1/4 cups all-purpose flour
3/4 teaspoon baking soda
1/2 teaspoons salt
1 cup pecans or walnuts,
    coarsely chopped

Preheat your griddle. Combine the banana, egg, buttermilk and oil in a large mixing bowl. Combine the flour, baking soda and salt in a medium bowl. Heat a griddle over medium heat until evenly heated. Add the dry ingredients to the wet ingredients and stir until just blended. Batter will be lumpy. Gently stir in the nuts. Oil the griddle (if necessary). Drop batter by 1/3 cupfuls onto the hot griddle. When bubbles form on top of pancakes, flip them over and cook the other side. Pancakes should be golden.

Serve with Spiced Syrup and Organic Chicken Apple Sausages from Panizzera Meats in Occidental.

Spiced Syrup:

1/2 cup sugar
1 tablespoon cornstarch
1 1/2 teaspoons ground cinnamon
1/2 teaspoon grated nutmeg
1/2 teaspoon salt

1/2 cup water
3 tablespoons fresh lemon juice
1 teaspoon vanilla extract
2 tablespoons butter

In a medium saucepan, stir together sugar, cornstarch, cinnamon, nutmeg and salt until well blended with no lumps of cornstarch. Add water and lemon juice and cook, stirring constantly, over medium heat. When syrup boils, it will thicken and clarify slightly. Remove from heat and add vanilla and butter. Keep stirring until butter is blended in.

Serves: 4

Double Corn Muffins

1 cup corn flour (masa)
1 tablespoon sugar
1 1/8 teaspoons baking powder
3/8 teaspoon salt
Dash black pepper
3/4 cup milk
1/3 cup vegetable oil
1 egg
1/2 cup fresh corn, cut from the cob

Preheat oven to 400 degrees Fahrenheit.

Mix together masa, sugar, baking powder, salt and pepper in large mixing bowl. In smaller bowl, whisk the egg, then add oil and milk, and stir. Pour wet mixture into large bowl and mix with dry ingredients. If batter is stiff, add more milk until it is pourable consistency. Stir in corn. Grease 6 large muffin cups. Fill cups to almost full. Bake for 15 to 18 minutes, or until set. These are better if you do not overbake them.

Serves: 6

Eggs Benedict

12 eggs
1 1/2 cups coarse bread crumbs
12 slices of ham, cut round
Red bell pepper and pine nuts, to garnish

Julienne the red bell pepper and then cut into "confetti." Toast pine nuts. Set aside. Sprinkle 1/4 cup bread crumbs on each of six dinner plates. Heat ham rounds. Poach eggs until whites are set, about 4 minutes. Place two ham rounds over bread crumbs on each plate. Gently place poached eggs atop ham. Top with Hollandaise sauce and garnish with red bell pepper confetti and toasted pine nuts.

Serves: 6 (two eggs each)

Blender Hollandaise Sauce

3 egg yolks (save whites for another purpose)
1 tablespoon fresh squeezed lemon juice
1 teaspoon Dijon mustard
1 cup butter

Drop egg yolks in blender. Add the lemon juice and mustard. Heat butter over medium heat until it boils, stirring constantly so it does not brown. Whirl first three ingredients until blended. With blender running, slowly add piping hot butter. This will splatter, so cover blender top with a tea towel. When butter is all added, sauce will be thick enough not to splatter. Watch blending process until sauce reaches desired consistency. Serve immediately.

Serves: 6

Lemon Blueberry Scones

3 cups all-purpose flour
1/3 cup granulated sugar
2 1/2 teaspoons baking powder
1/2 teaspoon baking soda
3/4 teaspoon salt
3/4 cup cold butter, cut into pieces
3/4 cup dried blueberries
Zest from one small lemon
3/4 cup buttermilk
1 tablespoon cream

Preheat oven to 425 degrees Fahrenheit.

Stir together dry ingredients. Add butter pieces and blend together with pastry blender or Kitchenaid mixer until mixture resembles coarse crumbs. Zest the lemon over the bowl. Add the dried blueberries and mix together. Add buttermilk and mix until dough forms a ball. Turn out onto floured board. Press or roll into a round about 3/4 inch thick. Cut into wedges. Place on ungreased baking sheet. Brush with cream. Bake 11 to 14 minutes until lightly browned. Cool slightly before removing from baking sheet.

Optional: To glaze the scones, mix juice of the lemon with about 2 cups of confectioner's sugar, enough to make the glaze thick but spreadable. Smooth glaze over scones when almost cool.

Yield: 8 to 12

Quick Drop Biscuits

These are super easy and fast - basic ingredients, no rolling, no kneading, no pricking, no waiting!

    2 cups all-purpose flour
    2 teaspoons baking powder
    1 teaspoon salt
    1 egg
    1/3 cup vegetable oil
    2/3 cup milk

Heat oven to 400 degrees Fahrenheit.

Stir together dry ingredients. Whisk egg in large bowl. Add milk and oil and stir. Add dry ingredients to egg and stir just to blend. Drop by large spoonfuls onto greased baking sheet. Bake for 12 to 15 minutes, or until biscuits are set and tinged with brown.

Yield: 6 to 8

Welcome home! This beautiful 1915 historic country estate is located in the heart of the Valley of the Moon. Sit on the wrap-around porch and gaze out at the beautiful vineyards and mountains.

Furnished in Craftsman-style furnishings, the parlors and guest rooms are comfortable and welcoming, reflecting the beauty of our natural surroundings. Enjoy a full gourmet breakfast using fresh locally grown produce. Your hosts are available to assist with recommendations for exceptional wine tasting and dining experiences.

Birmingham Bed & Breakfast

www.birminghambb.com
707-833-6996 • 800-819-1388
8790 Highway 12 • Kenwood, CA 95452

Signature Recipe

Birmingham Eggs

1 cup half and half
4 eggs (1 egg per serving)
1/2 cup all-purpose flour
1/4 teaspoon dried basil
1/8 teaspoon garlic power
1/8 teaspoon pepper
1/8 teaspoon salt
4 white onions, finely diced
1/2 cup sliced black olives
3/4 cup diced ham, Canadian bacon or cooked chicken sausage (may be omitted)
1 cup shredded Italian cheese (I use a blend with Asiago)
1/2 cup diced tomato for topping

In blender, combine half and half, eggs, flour, basil, garlic powder, pepper, and salt; blend until smooth. Spray 4 large ramekins or custard cups with nonstick cooking spray. Layer green onions, black olives, ham, and cheese in ramekins. Pour egg mixture into ramekins. Cover and refrigerate overnight.

Preheat oven to 325 degrees Fahrenheit.

Remove ramekins from refrigerator. Uncover and bake 20 minutes. Increase temperature to 350 and continue baking for 10 minutes. Sprinkle with diced tomato; bake 5 to 10 minutes longer or until set. Garnish with green onion and diced tomatoes if desired.

Serves: 4

Baked Apples

Serve these as a breakfast first course, or as dessert with a scoop of vanilla ice cream.

> 4 Granny Smith apples, peeled, cored, sliced or chopped
> Brown sugar, enough to cover bottom of baking dish
> Cinnamon, nutmeg, cloves

Preheat oven to 350 degrees Fahrenheit.

Place apple slices in bowl and toss with water and lemon juice. Drain apples and pat dry.

Cover bottom of baking dish with brown sugar; sprinkle cinnamon, nutmeg and cloves over sugar. Add apples and turn to coat. Top with small pats of butter.

Bake for 20 to 25 minutes, stirring once during baking. Serve warm in individual dishes, topped with cinnamon.

Serves: 4

Broiled Blueberries

An easy and elegant addition to complement a pancake or French toast entrée.

3 cups fresh blueberries
1 cup sour cream
1 teaspoon vanilla extract
Brown sugar

Preheat oven to broil.

Divide blueberries evenly among 6 small ramekins or custard cups (1/2 cup). In small bowl, mix sour cream and vanilla; spoon over berries. Sprinkle with brown sugar (removing any lumps). Broil 2 minutes or until sugar caramelizes (watch carefully).

Note: Blackberries, sliced strawberries, or a combination of firm berries are also delicious.

Serves: 6

Chili Cheese Puff

This is an excellent brunch dish; serve with our Stuffed Tomatoes.

12 eggs
1/2 cup of all-purpose flour, unsifted
1 teaspoon baking powder
1/2 teaspoon salt
1/4 teaspoon black pepper
1 pint (16 ounces) low fat small curd cottage cheese
2 pounds jack cheese, shredded
1/2 cup butter, melted
3 dashes of hot sauce
1 8-ounce can diced mild green chilies
1 4-ounce jar diced pimentos

In the bowl of an electric mixer beat the eggs until light and lemon-colored. Add flour, baking powder, salt, black pepper, cottage cheese, jack cheese, and melted butter, blending until smooth. Stir in the chilies and pimentos. Pour mixture into two 9-inch pie pans sprayed with cooking spray. Cover with plastic wrap and refrigerate overnight.

The next morning, set out at room temperature for 30 minutes.

Preheat oven to 350 degrees Fahrenheit.

Bake uncovered for about 50 to 60 minutes or until top is browned and center appears puffed and firm. Let set 10 to 15 minutes before serving. Top with a dollop of sour cream and chopped parsley.

Serves: 10 to 12

Italian Easter Pie

A family recipe served traditionally at Easter brunch.

Filling:

3 pounds Italian sausage, cooked, drained and cooled
3 pounds ricotta cheese
3 eggs
Chopped parsley
Pepper to taste
1/2 cup grated Parmesan Reggiano cheese

Mix together cheese, 3 eggs, parsley, salt and pepper. Add cooled sausage and mix.

Dough:

3 eggs
1/2 cup oil
1 cup milk
5 cups flour
3 teaspoons baking powder
1 teaspoon salt
1 tablespoon sugar
Egg wash (egg mixed with a little milk or water)

Preheat oven to 400 degrees Fahrenheit.

Beat eggs, stir in oil and add milk. Sift dry ingredients and add gradually to egg mixture. Knead until smooth. Place dough in warm bowl for 15 minutes. Divide dough into two balls; roll out 1 ball to fit medium jellyroll pan and place on greased pan. Spread filling over dough. Roll out rest of dough and place on top of filling. Brush top with egg wash. Bake for 30 minutes. Reduce temperature to 300 degrees and bake until golden brown, approximately 15 to 20 minutes.

Serves: up to 16 depending on size of slices

Peach Soup

2 1/2 to 3 cups sliced peaches (4 fresh peeled peaches, about 1 1/2
   pounds, or one 16-ounce bag frozen peaches)
2 tablespoons sugar, more to taste
2 tablespoons plain nonfat yogurt or sour cream
2 cups orange juice
Generous dash of cinnamon
1 banana

In blender, puree all of the ingredients until smooth. Serve at once or
refrigerate until ready to serve. Garnish with spring of mint.

Variation: Add 2 cups of chopped cantaloupe in place of banana.

Serves 4 to 6

Stuffed Tomatoes

This is an excellent side for any egg dish.

   4 medium or large tomatoes
   Balsamic vinegar
   Salt and pepper to taste
   1/2 cup breadcrumbs
   1/4 cup unsweetened butter
   1/2 cup freshly grated Parmesan
   2 tablespoons freshly chopped Italian parsley
   1 teaspoon dried basil
   1/2 teaspoon garlic powder

Preheat oven to 350 degrees Fahrenheit if cooking immediately.

Cut tomatoes in half and core; brush small amount of balsamic vinegar inside each tomato and sprinkle with a little salt and pepper. Melt butter and allow to slightly cool. Mix dried ingredients and stir into melted butter until coated. Spoon mixture into tomatoes.

May be made ahead: cover with plastic wrap and refrigerate overnight. Remove from refrigerator and allow to sit for 15 minutes.

Bake for 20 to 25 minutes, until tops are golden.

To serve, create a "bed" of spring greens, drizzle with balsamic reduction, and nestle tomato half in the greens.

Serves: 8

Rejuvenate at this charming Victorian Inn located two blocks from the historic Healdsburg plaza. The Camellia Inn delivers traditional romance, grace and style with contemporary amenities including wireless Internet access. Lucy Lewand, a second-generation innkeeper, manages the inn well known for more then 50 species of camellias, charming pool area, delightful rooms, insider Wine Country knowledge, innovative specials, family-friendly attributes and Chocolate Covered Wednesdays.

Home-style breakfast dishes are prepared daily to complement seasonal fresh fruits, fresh breads, pastries, home-blended granola and smoothies.

Camellia Inn

www.camelliainn.com

707-433-8182 • 800-727-8182

211 North Street • Healdsburg, CA 95448

Signature Recipe

Apple Ham Breakfast Bread Pudding

The sweet and savory taste of this dish will delight your guests.

> 1 loaf day-old French bread, crusts removed and cut into 1 to 2-inch cubes
> 2 cups milk
> 7 eggs
> 1 teaspoon salt
> 1/2 cup sugar
> 1 apple, chopped
> 1 cup ham, diced
> 1/2 cup butter, melted
> 1/2 cup sugar
> 2 tablespoons maple syrup

Preheat oven to 350 degrees Fahrenheit.

Spread bread cubes on bottom of 9x12-inch greased casserole dish. Sprinkle ham and apples on top of the bread cubes. Mix together milk, eggs, sugar, and salt and pour over bread. Can be covered and refrigerated overnight.

Bake for 45-60 minutes. If top begins to get too brown, cover with foil.

Mix together melted butter and sugar until sugar is dissolved, add maple syrup and pour over warm bread pudding.

Yield: 12 to 18 pieces

Baked Brie and Tomato Breakfast Strata

We discovered this recipe during the summer of 2009 when we had an amazing intern who loved to cook, and an abundance of heirloom tomatoes and leftover French bread. With these ingredients – what's not to like?

   2 small zucchini, cut crosswise into 1/4-inch slices (2 cups)
   6 1/2-inch thick slices crusty sourdough bread
   8 ounces Brie cheese, cut into 1/2-inch cubes
   4 Roma or Heirloom tomatoes, cut lengthwise into 1/4-inch slices
   3 eggs
   2/3 cup evaporated skim milk
   1/3 cup finely chopped onion
   3 tablespoons snipped fresh dill
   1/2 teaspoon salt
   1/8 teaspoon pepper
   6 to 8 cherry tomatoes
   Nonstick cooking spray

Cook the zucchini, covered, in a small amount of boiling, lightly salted water for 2 to 3 minutes or until just tender. Drain and set aside.

Spray a 9x13-inch glass baking dish with nonstick cooking spray. Arrange bread slices in the prepared baking dish, cutting as necessary to fit. Sprinkle half of the Brie evenly on top. Arrange zucchini and tomatoes on top of bread. Sprinkle with remaining cheese. In a bowl, combine eggs, evaporated skim milk, onion, dill, salt, and pepper. Pour evenly over vegetables and cheese. Lightly press vegetables down with the back of a spoon to be sure everything is saturated with egg mixture. Cover with plastic wrap; chill for 4 to 24 hours.

Preheat oven to 325 degrees Fahrenheit.

Remove plastic wrap from strata; cover with foil. Bake for 30 minutes. Uncover and bake for 25 to 30 minutes more or until knife inserted near the center comes out clean. Let stand for 10 minutes before serving.

Serves: 8 to 12

Citrus Mini Cakes

These little cakes are delicious and freeze well. The recipe makes a lot so they're good for a crowd.

    1 package (18 1/4 ounces) yellow cake mix
    1 1/4 cups water
    3 eggs
    1/3 cup vegetable oil
    3 1/2 cups confectioners' sugar
    1/2 cup orange juice
    1/4 cup lemon juice
    Toasted chopped almonds

Preheat oven to 350 degrees Fahrenheit.

Grease well 3 miniature muffin pans.

In a mixing bowl, combine cake mix, water, eggs, and oil; beat on low speed for 30 seconds. Beat on medium speed for 2 minutes. Fill muffin cups two-thirds full. Bake for 10 to 12 minutes or until a toothpick inserted near the center comes out clean.

To make glaze, combine sugar and juices until smooth.

Cool cakes for 2 minutes; remove from pans. Immediately dip cakes into glaze, coating well. Place on wire racks and sprinkle tops with almonds.

Yield: 6 dozen

Farmer's Breakfast

A hearty main dish that you can add anything to from the fridge.

> 1 large bag frozen hash browns
> 2 cups diced ham or sausage
> 1/2 cup chopped green onions
> 1 1/2 cups grated pepper jack cheese (or your choice)
> Salt and pepper to season
> 8 eggs
> 2 cans evaporated milk (unsweetened)

Preheat oven to 350 degrees Fahrenheit.

Mix together all ingredients except eggs and milk and put in large greased heatproof casserole.

In another bowl, mix together eggs and milk. Pour over casserole. Bake for 1 hour.

Can be assembled and refrigerated overnight before baking.

Yield: 18 to 24 pieces

Lemon Chiffon Smoothie

1 1/2 cups of frozen lemon sorbet
1 container of lemon chiffon low-fat yogurt
1/2 cup milk
Fresh lemon slices for garnish

Combine all ingredients in blender or food processor until well blended. Pour into chilled glasses.

Note: Vanilla yogurt or ice cream can be substituted with lemon juice added to taste. This recipe also makes wonderful popsicles.

Serves: 2

Muffins That Taste Like Donuts

2/3 cup shortening (or butter)
2 eggs
1 cup sugar
3 cups flour
3 teaspoons baking powder
1/2 teaspoon salt
1/2 teaspoon nutmeg
1 cup milk
1 1/2 sticks of butter, melted
1 cup sugar
1/2 teaspoon cinnamon
1/2 teaspoon mace

Preheat oven to 375 degrees Fahrenheit.

Grease muffins tins. Beat together shortening, sugar, and eggs. Combine dry ingredients and add to shortening mix. Pour in milk and mix well. Fill muffin tins 2/3 full. Bake for 20 minutes.

Combine sugar, cinnamon and mace in a shallow dish. While the muffins are still hot, dip them in melted butter and then the sugar mixture.

Yield: 24

Rich Chocolate Bundt Cake

've been making this cake for more than 30 years and it's a chocolate lover's delight.

 1 package Duncan Hines Deep Chocolate cake mix
 1 small package instant chocolate pudding
 1/2 cup vegetable oil
 1/2 cup warm water
 1 cup (1/2 pint) sour cream
 4 eggs
 1 package (12 ounces) chocolate chips
 Confectioner's sugar

Preheat oven to 350 degrees Fahrenheit.

Mix all ingredients except for eggs, chocolate, and sugar. Add eggs one at a time. Beat well. Fold in the chocolate chips. Grease a bundt pan lightly and pour in mixture. Bake for 1 hour. Cool for 45 minutes and unmold. Sift confectioner's sugar over top. Do not refrigerate.

Yield: 20 pieces (because it's so rich)

Case Ranch Inn
Sonoma Wine Country Bed & Breakfast

Case Ranch Inn is your peaceful respite in a country location (on the quiet side of Healdsburg) ... a place where you can relax and enjoy the renowned Russian River Valley wine country and its many beautiful attractions. This Victorian farmhouse, circa 1894, sits on two acres on a quiet country road. With three guest suites in the main house, Case Ranch Inn captures the intimacy of a traditional bed and breakfast. All rooms have queen beds featuring luxury pillow-top mattresses, spacious ensuite bathrooms, luxury robes and amenities. Serving full country breakfast using natural and organic ingredients. $185-$215.

Case Ranch Inn
www.caseranchinn.com
707-887-8711 • 877-887-8711
7446 Poplar Drive • Forestville, CA 95436

Signature Recipe

Fiesta Frittata

Our guests consistently praise this, especially when we use chile peppers from our garden. We love it because it is so simple to prepare. It tastes great with roasted potatoes, sausage and salsa on the side.

- 10 eggs, lightly beaten
- 1/2 cup all-purpose flour
- 1 teaspoon baking powder
- 1/2 teaspoon chile powder
- 1/2 teaspoon cumin powder
- 1 tablespoon vegetable oil
- 2 cups small curd non-fat cottage cheese
- 1/2 pound grated Pepper Jack cheese (or combine Pepper Jack with Monterey Jack to equal 1/2 pound)
- 2 cups chopped mild chile peppers, any combination of various colored mild peppers, sautéed in oil until al dente and cooled (or use three 4-ounce cans of diced green chiles).

Preheat oven to 350 degrees Fahrenheit.

Butter or lightly oil a 9x13-inch shallow baking dish. Whisk together flour, baking powder and spices. Add eggs and oil, blending well. Blend in remaining ingredients. Pour mixture into the prepared baking dish and bake for 35 to 45 minutes, or until set. Check by inserting a knife or toothpick, which should come out dry. Let stand for about 5 minutes, then cut into squares and serve hot.

Serves: 8 to 10

Baked Pears with Granola

4 ripe D'Anjou pears, or any other pear in season
1/2 cup granola
1/4 cup orange juice
2 tablespoons butter
Ground cinnamon
Ground cloves
Ground nutmeg
6-ounce container of vanilla yogurt

Preheat oven to 350 degrees Fahrenheit.

Slice pears in half, removing cores and stems. Evenly spread granola in bottom of glass baking dish. Place pears cut side down on top of granola. Pour orange juice over pears and evenly distribute melted butter over each pear. Sprinkle lightly with cinnamon and nutmeg, and then add a pinch of cloves to each pear.

Bake for about 30 minutes (depending on ripeness of the pears) until pears are tender. Pierce gently with a fork to test for firmness. Place each in a small bowl and top with a teaspoon of yogurt and a sprig of mint.

Serves: 8

Broiled Figs with Raspberry Sauce

Since fresh figs are fairly costly, we only serve this when our fig tree is in season. Our guests consider this a special gourmet treat, especially when we also use our fresh raspberries for the sauce.

24 fresh figs
Sugar
Small container vanilla yogurt

Preheat oven broiler.

Rinse figs, remove any remaining stem and cut in half lengthwise. Place the halves on a lightly oiled cookie sheet and sprinkle with sugar (about 1/8 teaspoon or less each). Broil for a few minutes until they have spread open and are hot. Watch carefully to make sure they don't overcook.

Spoon 1 teaspoon of raspberry sauce on each plate, spreading it out a bit. Arrange 4 halves on each plate and top each grouping of 4 with 2 more halves (total of 6 fig halves per plate). Place a teaspoon dollop of vanilla yogurt on top and finish off with a sprig of fresh mint.

Raspberry Sauce:

1 cup fresh or 5 ounces unsweetened frozen raspberries, thawed.
2 tablespoons sugar, or to taste

In a blender combine the raspberries and sugar, blending to a smooth sauce. Strain the sauce through a fine-meshed sieve. Store in an airtight container in the refrigerator up to a week.

Serves: 8

Chocolate Chip Cookies

Apparently we have many cookie monsters staying at our inn! They exclaim over these cookies and love the fact that they are homemade. The cookies freeze very well for several weeks.

    3 cups all-purpose unbleached flour
    1 teaspoon baking soda
    1 teaspoon salt
    1/2 cup granulated sugar
    1 1/2 cups brown sugar
    1/2 cup butter, softened
    1/2 cup vegetable oil
    1 1/2 teaspoons vanilla
    1 cup semi-sweet chocolate chips
    3/4 cup pecans, chopped

Preheat oven to 375 degrees Fahrenheit.

Lightly grease baking sheets. Whisk together flour, baking soda, and salt. Beat together sugars, butter, oil, eggs and vanilla in large mixing bowl at medium speed about 30 seconds. Stop and scrape down sides of bowl and then beat at high speed for 30 seconds more. Stop and scrape down bowl again. At low speed gradually beat in flour mixture for 2 minutes. Turn to medium speed and beat about 30 seconds more. Add chocolate chips and nuts and mix at low speed about 15 seconds, until chips and nuts are well incorporated into batter.

Drop by rounded teaspoonfuls on greased baking sheets, about 2 inches apart. Bake for 10 to 12 minutes. Remove from baking sheets immediately and cool on wire racks.

Yield: 4 dozen

Lemon Oat Bran Pancakes

These pancakes are good enough to eat without maple syrup. Repeat guests especially request these pancakes. The lemon zest really makes the lemon flavor stand out.

  1 1/2 cups all-purpose flour
  1/2 cup oat bran
  1 tablespoon sugar
  2 teaspoons baking powder
  1 teaspoon baking soda
  1/2 teaspoon salt, or to taste
  2 eggs
  3 tablespoons melted butter or vegetable oil
  2 tablespoons fresh lemon juice
  2 teaspoons grated lemon rind
  1 3/4 cups milk

In a large bowl, whisk together the flour, oat bran, sugar, baking powder, baking soda and salt. In a medium bowl, beat the eggs. Beat in the butter or oil, lemon juice and lemon rind. Beat in the milk. Add the milk mixture to the dry ingredients and stir until fairly smooth; let stand 5 minutes.

Heat a skillet or griddle over medium-high heat until a drop of water dances across the surface of the pan before evaporating. If not using a non-stick surface griddle or pan, brush the surface lightly with butter or oil. For each pancake, drop 1/4 cup of batter onto the cooking surface. Cook until bubbles start to burst on the top; turn and cook until golden on the bottom.

Variation: Blueberry-Lemon Pancakes: stir about 1 cup blueberries into the batter.

Yield: 15 to 18 4 1/4-inch pancakes.

Sour Cream Pancakes

During the summer season we put fresh raspberries from our garden in the batter. From the kitchen I can hear the oohs and ahhs, especially when we serve the pancakes with fresh-pressed juice made with apples from our orchard.

- 3/4 cup all-purpose flour
- 1/2 cup whole wheat pastry flour
- 1 tablespoon sugar
- 2 teaspoons baking powder
- 1 teaspoon baking soda
- 1/2 teaspoon salt
- 1 egg
- 1 cup milk
- 1/2 cup sour cream
- 1 1/2 teaspoons vanilla

In a large bowl, stir together both flours, the sugar, baking powder, baking soda and salt. In a medium bowl, beat the egg. Stir in the milk, sour cream and vanilla. Add the milk mixture to the dry ingredients and stir until just combined. The batter may have some lumps.

Heat a skillet or griddle over medium heat until a drop of water dances across the surface of the pan before evaporating. If not using a non-stick surface, brush the skillet with butter or oil. For each pancake, drop 2 to 3 tablespoons of batter onto the skillet. Cook until one or two bubbles start to burst on the top; turn and cook until golden on the bottom.

Variation:
Stir in1/2 cup blueberries or raspberries.

Yield: 12
3 1/2-inch pancakes

Zucchini Basil Frittata

This is another tasty treat for our guests with the fresh zucchini and basil from our garden. We garnish with a sprig of fresh basil on the frittata and accompany with roasted potatoes and sausage.

> 10 eggs, lightly beaten
> 1/2 cup all-purpose flour
> 1 teaspoon baking powder
> 1 tablespoon vegetable oil
> 2 teaspoons olive oil
> 2 cups diced zucchini squash
> 2 cups small curd non-fat cottage cheese
> 1/2 cup fresh basil, chopped (or 2 tablespoons dried)
> 1/2 pound grated Monterey Jack cheese

Preheat oven to 350 degrees Fahrenheit.

Butter or lightly oil a 9-by-13-inch shallow baking dish. Heat 2 teaspoons of olive oil in large skillet over medium heat. Add zucchini to oil and sauté for several minutes, stirring so it does not brown. Turn off heat and allow to cool. Mix flour and baking powder. Add eggs and oil, blending well. Blend in remaining ingredients, gradually adding and incorporating warm zucchini. Put mixture into the prepared baking dish and bake for 35 to 45 minutes, or until set. Check by inserting a knife or toothpick, which should come out dry. Let stand for about 5 minutes, then cut into squares and serve hot.

Serves: 8 to 10

A Wine Country Bed & Breakfast providing affordable elegance. We are dedicated to providing wine country visitors with the utmost in gracious hospitality and comfortable lodging.

English Tea Garden Inn

www.teagardeninn.com

707-894-8557 • 800-996-8675

119 West Third Street • Cloverdale, CA 95425

Signature Recipe

Frittata Primavera

2 tablespoons olive oil
1 small red potato, cubed
1 stalk of celery, trimmed and sliced
1/2 green bell pepper, trimmed and diced
1/2 yellow onion, peeled and diced
6 large eggs, well beaten
Salt and pepper, to taste

Preheat oven to 475 degrees Fahrenheit.

Heat oil in 10-inch ovenproof skillet. Add potato and celery pieces and sauté until lightly browned. Add onion and green pepper and cook until all vegetables are soft and lightly browned. Add beaten eggs, sprinkle with salt and pepper and cook a minute or two, until frittata is browned on the bottom. Place skillet in oven and bake 5 to 8 minutes until puffy and golden. Remove from oven and cut into quarters. Serve with sour cream or hot sauce if desired.

Serves: 4

Orange Current Scones

These fruit-laced scones are reminiscent of traditional English teatime treats. Here, you prepare a quick orange butter to spread on top for an extra dose of tangy citrus flavor and a rich buttery taste.

   About 3 cups all-purpose flour
   About 3/4 cup sugar
   1/2 teaspoon baking powder
   1 teaspoon baking soda
   2 teaspoons grated orange peel
   1/2 cup (1/4 pound) cold butter or margarine cut into pieces
   3/4 cup dried currants
   3/4 cup buttermilk

Preheat oven to 400 degrees Fahrenheit.

Mix flour, sugar, baking powder, baking soda and orange peel in large bowl. With pastry blender or 2 knives, cut in butter until mixture resembles fine crumbs. Stir in currants. Add buttermilk and stir until evenly moistened.

Turn dough out onto a lightly floured board and knead until smooth (about 10 turns). Pat into a 9-inch round and place in a greased 9-inch-round cake pan. Sprinkle lightly with sugar. Bake about 40 minutes or until golden brown. Turn scones out onto a rack; invert onto a serving plate. Cut into 8 wedges.

Serve warm or at room temperature with flavored butter.

Orange Butter

   1/2 cup (1/4 pound) butter or margarine, at room temperature
   1 teaspoon grated orange peel
   1 tablespoon powdered sugar

In small bowl combine ingredients and beat until creamy and smooth. Makes about 1/2 cup.

Servings: 8

Potato Cheddar Mushroom Egg Bake

This dish can be made the night before and kept in the refrigerator to bake in the morning.

8 frozen hash brown patties
1 package, (8 ounces) sliced fresh mushrooms
1/2 cup sliced green onions
3 cups (16 ounces) shredded cheddar cheese
7 eggs
1 cup milk
1/2 teaspoon salt
1/2 teaspoon ground mustard

Place hash brown patties in a single layer in a greased 13x9-inch baking dish. Cover with mushrooms and green onions. Sprinkle with shredded cheddar cheese. In a bowl, beat eggs, milk, salt and mustard. Pour over casserole. Cover with foil and refrigerate overnight.

Remove from refrigerator at least 30 minutes before baking.

Preheat oven to 350 degrees Fahrenheit.

Bake covered for 1 hour. Uncover; bake 15 minutes longer or until edges are golden brown and a knife inserted near the center comes out clean.

Serves: 8

Puffed Oven-baked Pancake

This recipe is for one individual pancake. For each serving use a 4-inch diameter, shallow, ovenproof baking dish. Top with a generous sprinkling of powdered sugar and a squeeze of lemon or lime. Or use fresh berries, sliced seasonal fruit, maple syrup or any other desired topping.

- 1 tablespoon unsalted butter
- 1 large egg
- 1/4 cup milk
- 1/4 cup all-purpose flour
- 1/8 teaspoon salt
- 1 teaspoon sugar

Preheat oven to 475 degrees Fahrenheit.

Spray sides of baking dish generously with cooking spray. Place butter in bottom of dish and heat in microwave until the butter is melted and the container is hot.

In a blender, combine the egg, milk, flour, salt and sugar and blend until smooth. Put the baking dish on a cookie sheet and pour the batter into the dish. Place cookie sheet in oven and bake until the pancake is well puffed and golden, about 12 minutes, or longer for larger pancakes or those with a thicker layer of batter.

Serves: 1

Strawberry Banana French Toast

1 loaf French bread
5 eggs
3/4 cup milk
1/4 teaspoon baking powder
1 tablespoon vanilla extract
1 16-ounce bag frozen strawberries
4 ripe bananas, sliced
1 cup sugar
1 tablespoon apple pie spice
Cinnamon sugar

Cut the French bread into 8 thick slices. Combine the eggs, milk, baking powder and vanilla extract. Pour over bread. Cover and refrigerate overnight.

Preheat oven to 450 degrees Fahrenheit.

In the morning, combine the strawberries, bananas, sugar and apple pie spice. Spread fruit mixture in greased 9x13-inch baking dish and top with the prepared bread slices. Sprinkle with cinnamon sugar. Bake for 25 minutes.

To serve, place 1 slice of French bread on plate and spoon fruit sauce from the baking dish over top.

Serves: 8

Strawberry Muffins

1 1/2 cup rolled oats
3 cups flour
1 1/4 cups sugar
2 1/4 tablespoons baking powder
1 2/3 teaspoon salt
1 1/4 teaspoon baking soda
1 pint chopped fresh strawberries
3 eggs, slightly beaten
1 1/2 teaspoons almond extract
2 1/4 cups buttermilk
1 stick (1/4 pound) butter or margarine, melted
1/4 cup sugar
2 tablespoons cinnamon for topping

Preheat oven to 375 degrees Fahrenheit.

Grease or spray muffin tins. Combine oats, flour, sugar, baking powder, salt and baking soda. Add chopped strawberries. Mix together eggs, almond extract, buttermilk and butter, and add to flour mixture until dry ingredients are moistened. Fill greased muffin cups 2/3 full. Mix together sugar and cinnamon and sprinkle on top of muffins. Bake for 15 minutes or until done.

Yield: 36

Wine Country Baked Bananas

1/2 cup fresh orange juice
1/2 cup white wine
1/4 cup honey
1 1/2 teaspoons grated orange rind
1/4 teaspoon cinnamon
1/4 teaspoon nutmeg
6 medium bananas
1/4 cup finely chopped almonds (optional)
2 tablespoons butter or margarine (optional)

Preheat oven to 350 degrees Fahrenheit.

In a small saucepan, combine juice, wine, honey, orange rind, cinnamon and nutmeg. Heat until warm. Peel bananas and split in half, lengthwise. Place bananas, cut side down, in a greased baking dish large enough to accommodate them without crowding. Pour warm sauce over bananas. Sprinkle with almonds and dot with butter, if desired.

Bake for a total of 25 minutes, basting bananas with sauce after the first 15 minutes.

Serves: 6

Nestled among ancient oak trees in the enchanted village of Glen Ellen, this California Bed & Breakfast inn is ideal for romantic escapes, honeymoons, family getaways, wine touring, spa treatments and the serenity of the Valley of the Moon.

A year at a culinary school in her mother's native Norway and twenty years as an innkeeper have established Kristi as a great favorite of locals and visitors. The bounty of Sonoma County and the appeal of country and ethnic tastes have sparked the creation of many original recipes and a variety of popular cooking classes.

Glenelly Inn & Cottages

www.glenelly.com
707-996-6720
5131 Warm Springs Road • Glen Ellen, CA 95442

Signature Recipe

Southwestern Quiche

Crust

2 to 3 very thin large flour tortillas (Jalisco brand are made fresh here in Sonoma)

Lime-infused olive oil (I use Figone's from here in Glen Ellen)

Spray a 9-inch pie pan with cooking spray or brush lightly with olive oil or butter. Lay the tortillas in the pan, overlapping a little and extending the edges above the sides of the pan. Brush the tortillas with olive oil.

Filling

2 zucchini or yellow squash, coarsely diced

1 tomato, chopped

1/2 can corn kernels drained well, or kernels from one fresh ear of raw corn

1/2 cup chopped peppers (jalapenos or whatever you like, mild or spicy)

Green and pink pepper, freshly ground

Cumin, ground and/or seeds

Paprika and cayenne

1 cup cheese (any combination of Cotija, queso fresco, cheddar, jack), grated

6 eggs, beaten

1/2 cup buttermilk

Preheat oven to 400 degrees Fahrenheit.

Season the vegetables with salt, peppers, cumin, paprika and cayenne – all to taste. Saute in lime olive oil until soft but not mushy. Lay the vegetables evenly into the pan with the tortillas. Spread cheese evenly on top. Mix together eggs and buttermilk. Pour egg mixture over the top, and sprinkle with a little cayenne pepper.

Bake for 40 minutes or until set and golden. Let cool slightly, cut into wedges to serve. Garnish with avocado slices, fresh lime and fresh cilantro.

Note: I usually serve chorizo on the side, but you could put it into the quiche as well.

Serves: 6

Cornflake Buttermilk French Toast

This recipe was adapted from James Beard's famous French toast recipe, which I absolutely love!

    1/2 loaf sweet French bread
    2 sticks butter, melted
    8 to 9 large eggs
    1 quart buttermilk
    1/2 cup brown sugar
    1 tablespoon cinnamon (more if you want)
    1 cup crushed cornflakes

Butter a 9x13-inch baking dish using some of the melted butter. Cube the French bread into 1/4 to 1-inch cubes, and lay in baking dish. Pour 1 stick of the melted butter over the bread. Mix the eggs, buttermilk, sugar and cinnamon together and pour over the bread mixture. At this point, you can cover and refrigerate the dish up to 1 day ahead.

Preheat oven to 400 degrees Fahrenheit when ready to bake.

Let dish come to room temperature.

Spread the crushed cornflakes over the top and pour remaining 1 stick of melted butter evenly over the cornflakes. Bake approximately 45 minutes until top is golden and custard is set. Cut into squares.

Serve with an assortment of Kozlowski fruit syrups – especially apple and berry - and bacon, ham or sausage on the side.

Serves: 6 to 9

Espresso Coffee Cake
AKA Kaelene's Kona Coffee Cake

1 stick butter, melted
4 eggs
1 cup sour cream
1 package yellow cake mix
1/2 cup brown sugar
1/2 cup instant coffee (espresso, regular or decaf)

Preheat oven to 375 degrees Fahrenheit.

Spray or grease a Bundt pan.

Beat eggs lightly, mix in butter and sour cream. Add cake mix, sugar and coffee and mix thoroughly BY HAND.

Pour into Bundt pan and bake 40 minutes. Let cool in pan for 5 to 10 minutes, then turn onto wire rack to cool completely before slicing. Dust with powdered sugar.

Serves: 8 to 12

Lavender Corn Muffins

1 1/2 cups all-purpose flour or sweet white sorghum flour
2/3 cup granulated sugar
1/2 cup yellow cornmeal
1 tablespoon baking powder
1/2 teaspoon salt
1 tablespoon dried lavender
1 tablespoon freshly ground pink peppercorns
1 1/4 cups milk
2 large eggs, lightly beaten
1/3 cup vegetable oil
2 tablespoons butter or margarine, melted

Preheat oven to 350 degrees Fahrenheit.

Grease or paper-line 18 to 20 muffin cups.

Combine flour, sugar, cornmeal, baking powder, salt, lavender and pink pepper in medium bowl. Combine milk, eggs, vegetable oil and butter in large bowl and mix well. Add flour mixture; stir just until blended. Fill prepared muffin cups 2/3 full.

Bake for 18 to 20 minutes or until wooden pick inserted in center comes out clean. Cool in pans on wire racks for 5 minutes; serve warm.

Yield: 18 to 20

Leek Tart

This is really good with citrus scones and fresh strawberry preserves or strawberry bread and fresh melon, perhaps wrapped with prosciutto.

- 9-inch piecrust
- 2 large leeks, washed and thinly sliced
- 1/2 to 1 smoked chicken and apple sausage or your favorite (optional), diced
- 5 eggs, well beaten
- 2/3 cup heavy cream
- Salt to taste
- White pepper, freshly ground
- Nutmeg, freshly grated
- 1 cup Gruyere, Swiss or Jarlsberg cheese, grated

Preheat oven to 375 degrees Fahrenheit.

Sauté leeks in butter on low heat for 10 to 15 minutes, until soft. Add diced sausage if you like. Mix eggs with cream, salt, pepper, and nutmeg. Add leeks and grated cheese and combine well. Pour into piecrust.

Bake 30 to 40 minutes, until the tart is puffed, golden, and set in the middle.

Grate a little more fresh nutmeg on top before serving.

Serves: 4 to 6

Moondance Lasagna (vegetarian)

I created this recipe several years ago for Dunbar School's annual fundraiser, the "Moondance", to satisfy requests for a vegetarian entrée which our French chef, Rich, was not interested in doing.

- 1 box lasagna noodles, cooked al dente
- 4 cups Béchamel sauce
- 1 cup spaghetti squash, shredded
- 2 cups variety of squashes - sugar pumpkin, butternut, acorn, zucchini, spaghetti - roasted with olive oil until tender but not mushy, cooled and cut into cubes

Two bags fresh spinach, lightly steamed, stems removed

Nutmeg, freshly grated, to taste

Parmesan, Romano, Asiago, Jarlsberg and Smoked Gouda cheeses, grated, 3-4 cups total

Fresh tarragon, sage and rosemary, chopped, to taste

Butter

Béchamel Sauce:

- 1 stick butter
- 1 cup of flour
- 4 cups heavy cream, 1/2 and 1/2 or milk (not low or nonfat)

Melt the butter, stir in flour to form a roux. Cook roux for a few minutes but do not allow to color. Slowly add heavy cream, 1/2 and 1/2 or milk to the roux stirring constantly to avoid lumps. Let simmer for a few minutes, whisking to avoid lumps. Add more liquid as necessary, but make the sauce thicker than you think it should be because it is easier to thin it when using it. Season to taste with salt and white pepper.

For meat-eaters, brown and add finely diced salt pork to the sauce if you like.

Preheat oven to 375 degrees Fahrenheit.

Grease 9x13-inch baking pan with olive oil or butter. Line with cooked lasagna noodles. Spread a layer of spaghetti squash evenly on the noodles and top with thick layer of cubed squashes, and a generous layer of shredded Gouda and Jarlsberg cheese. To 1/2 of béchamel sauce add chopped tarragon, sage and rosemary to taste and spread over the squash/cheese layers.

Lay down another layer of lasagna noodles. Mix steamed spinach with the remaining béchamel sauce, season with nutmeg to taste and spread evenly over the noodles. Add final layer of noodles, top with the grated Parmesan/Romano/Asiago, and dot with butter. Bake until bubbly and hot through approximately 40 minutes.

Serves: 8 generously

Norwegian Breakfast Crepes

2 eggs
1 to 1 1/4 cups flour
2 2/3 cups milk
1 teaspoon each chopped chives, dill, green onion, tarragon
Prosciutto or smoked salmon

In a bowl mix eggs, flour and half of the milk. Stir until smooth. Add remainder of the milk and mix well. Add herbs. Let batter rest 10 to 15 minutes.

If adding prosciutto or salmon to batter, chop coarsely. You can also serve slices on the side.

Heat a non-stick 10-inch skillet and add a small amount of butter or margarine. When foam subsides, pour in small amount of batter – approximately 1/2 to 1 tablespoon (enough to make a thin layer when pan is tilted from side to side). Cook until lightly golden brown and roll like a crepe on a warmed serving platter.

Serve with lingonberry and/or blueberry preserves on the side, sour cream, and slices of prosciutto or salmon if not added to batter.

Serves: 4

THE HIDDEN OAK INN, circa 1914, is an exquisite example of a California Craftsman Bungalow. Located one block from Sonoma's Historic Plaza, in the prestigious eastside residential neighborhood. The casual elegance of this traditional bed and breakfast reflects a time of serenity and beauty. Hosts: Don & Valerie Patterson

Hidden Oak Inn

www.hiddenoakinn.com
707-996-9863 • 877-996-9863
214 East Napa Street • Sonoma, CA 95476

Signature Recipe

Granola

5 cups Quaker oatmeal
1/2 cup wheat germ
1/2 cup raw sunflower seeds (not roasted)
1/4 cup flax seeds
3/4 cup chopped nuts (pecans, walnuts or sliced almonds)
1 cup unsweetened flaked coconut
Sprinkle of cinnamon (optional)

Mix together in a large bowl.

In a small pan mix together and heat until sugar melts:

1/2 cup oil
3/4 cup brown sugar
1/4 cup honey
1 teaspoon vanilla

Add to dry ingredients and mix well.

Preheat oven to 350 degrees Fahrenheit.

Spray two 13x9x2-inch pans and divide mixed ingredients between two pans. Bake for 20 minutes, stir and continue baking until lightly toasted, about another 15 minutes. Remove from oven and stir during cooling time. Allow to fully cool before storing in airtight container.

Serve layered in a yogurt and fruit parfait or in a bowl with milk.

Note: Make several baggies of the dry mixture to have ready to mix and bake when you run out.

Buttermilk Scones

These scones are positively delicious when served warm with jam!

- 3 cups flour
- 1/2 cup sugar
- 1 tablespoon baking powder
- 1/2 teaspoon baking soda
- 3/4 teaspoon salt
- 1 1/2 sticks (6 ounces) cold unsalted butter, cut into small pieces
- 1 cup buttermilk
- 1 tablespoon grated orange or lemon zest

Optional:
- 1/2 teaspoon culinary Orange oil or Lemon oil

For Brushing:
- 1/2 stick unsalted butter, melted

Sprinkle tops:
- 1/4 cup sugar

Preheat oven to 350 degrees Fahrenheit. Mix first five ingredients together. (I make up several zip lock bags of this mixture and keep on hand.) Add cold butter pieces and, using a pastry blender, work the butter into the dry ingredients until it resembles coarse cornmeal. Pour in buttermilk, zest, and oil and mix with a fork only until the ingredients are just moistened.

Make dough into a ball and knead on floured surface (about 12 turns). Cut dough in half (I divide into thirds to make smaller scones). Roll one piece of dough into 1/2-inch-thick circle, brush with melted butter and sprinkle with sugar. Cut the circle into six triangles (I use a pizza cutter, but you can also use a cookie cutter). Place scones on an ungreased baking sheet, and set aside while you complete dough.

Bake scones for 12-15 minutes, until very lightly browned. Transfer to rack and cool slightly.

If not eaten day of baking, freeze in airtight container and store for up to one month. To serve, defrost to room temperature and reheat on a baking sheet at 350 degrees Fahrenheit for 5 minutes.

Yield: 16 to 18

Croissant French Toast

8 medium croissants (or bear claws)
8 tablespoons peach jam or orange marmalade
8 eggs, beaten
1/4 cup orange juice
1 cup whipping cream or half and half
1 teaspoon almond extract (omit if using bear claws)
Garnish: confectioners' sugar and fresh fruit

The night before baking, grease a 13x9x2-inch baking pan or use 6-8 individual 8-ounce ramekins. Split croissants in half. Place bottom halves in pan.

Combine jam and orange juice and blend well. Pour 2/3 of jam mixture over croissants. Replace tops of croissants.

Blend together eggs, cream, and almond extract. Pour over croissants. Spoon remaining 1/3 jam mixture over croissants.

Cover with plastic wrap and store in the refrigerator for at least 8 hours before baking.

Preheat oven to 350 degrees Fahrenheit

Bake uncovered in center of oven for 40 to 45 minutes. Let stand 5 minutes before serving. Garnish with a dusting of confectioners' sugar and fresh fruit.

Serves: 8

Egg Cups

8 teaspoons butter (or cooking spray)
8 teaspoons heavy cream or half and half
8 eggs
8 teaspoons Parmesan cheese
Salt and pepper to taste
8 4-ounce ramekins

Preheat oven to 425 degrees Fahrenheit.

Spray each ramekin with non-stick cooking spray. In each ramekin, layer ingredients as follows: 1 teaspoon butter (or cooking spray), 1 tablespoon cream, one egg, 1 teaspoon cheese, salt and pepper. Bake for 7 to 10 minutes until yolk is desired doneness.

Note: For added flavor, include a little cooked prosciutto, bacon or spinach leaves after the cream.

Serves: 4 to 8 depending on a 1-egg or 2-egg serving. Put 1 egg per ramekin.

Potato Leek Frittata

3 tablespoons olive oil
6 to 8 small red potatoes, sliced
Salt and pepper to taste
2 leeks, white and light green portions, thinly sliced (wash well and soak in water after slicing)
10 eggs
1/2 cup heavy cream
3 ounces Gruyere cheese, shredded (may substitute Swiss)
1 tablespoon finely chopped fresh flat-leaf parsley

Preheat oven to 350 degrees Fahrenheit.

In a large skillet over medium high heat, add 1 tablespoon olive oil, leeks, salt and pepper and cook stirring occasionally, 6 to 8 minutes. Transfer to bowl to cool.

In same pan, add 1 tablespoon olive oil and potatoes, cover and cook flipping occasionally, about 8 minutes or until fork tender.

While potatoes are cooking, whisk eggs and cream together in a bowl. Stir in cheese, parsley, and leeks.

Using oven-safe pan (or cover handle of skillet with aluminum foil), add last tablespoon of olive oil and cover bottom of pan with potatoes. Pour egg and leek mixture over potatoes. Cook on medium heat until set around edges. Finish cooking in oven until middle is set and top is lightly browned.

Serves: 8

Strawberry Bread

3 cups flour
1 tablespoon cinnamon
1 teaspoon baking soda
1/2 teaspoon baking powder
1 teaspoon salt
1 cup oil
2 cups sugar
3 eggs
1 teaspoon vanilla
2 cups fresh strawberries, chopped
1 cup nuts, chopped (pecans are good)

Preheat oven to 350 degrees Fahrenheit.

Grease and flour two 4x8-inch loaf pans.

Combine first 5 ingredients in medium bowl. Beat together oil and sugar in mixing bowl. Add eggs one at a time, then vanilla and mix well. Gradually add dry ingredients to creamed mixture, mixing just until all ingredients are moistened. Stir in strawberries and nuts.

Spoon mixture into prepared loaf pans. Bake for 1 hour until a wooden toothpick inserted in center comes out clean. Cool in pans 10 minutes; remove to wire rack and cool.

Yield: 2 loaves

Tomato Puff Pastry Tart

1 box frozen puff pastry, thawed
1 large egg, lightly beaten
1/2 cup finely grated Parmesan cheese
1 pound Roma tomatoes, oven-dried *
2 teaspoons minced garlic
2 tablespoons olive oil
Salt and pepper
2 cups shredded mozzarella cheese
2 tablespoons chopped fresh basil

Preheat oven to 425 degrees Fahrenheit.

Dust work surface with flour. Unfold both pieces of puff pastry and roll into one large sheet and place on a parchment lined cookie sheet. Fold edges over about 1/2 inch and brush edges and bottom with beaten egg. Using a fork, poke holes in bottom of pastry and sprinkle with Parmesan cheese. Bake for 15 minutes and then reduce oven to 350 degrees and continue to bake for 15 minutes. When pastry is done, sprinkle with mozzarella cheese and place 1 pound of oven-dried tomatoes on top in neat rows.

Turn oven back up to 425 degrees.

In a small bowl, combine garlic, oil, and pinch of salt and pepper. Brush tomatoes with oil mixture. Bake until pastry is golden brown and the cheese is melted. Cool 5 minutes and sprinkle basil over top.

*Oven-dried tomatoes: Roma tomatoes work best, as they will hold their shape. This recipe only needs 1 pound of tomatoes, but because it takes several hours, I dry extra for another use.

Slice 2 pounds of tomatoes in half, deseed and prick skin several times with sharp knife. Lay slices cut side down on large baking sheet and place in 200 degree oven. Dry 3 to 6 hours or until your desired dryness (I leave a little moisture in them for the tart).

Tucked in the tiny hamlet of Geyserville, majestically stands these 2 incomparable inns "Where Wine & Romance Intertwine." Enjoy wine in the vineyard gazebo, under the grape arbors, or around the pool. Or, just stroll through the lovely gardens and vineyard.

Hope-Merrill Bed & Breakfast Inn

www.hope-inns.com

707-857-3356 • 800-825-4233

P.O. Box 42 • Geyserville, CA 95441

Signature Recipe # Chili Egg Puff Casserole

Over the years, this recipe has been a favorite among our guests. It is the most requested and has become our signature dish.

For 2 round quiche dishes:

10 eggs
1 pint creamed cottage cheese
1 pound Jack cheese with Jalapeno peppers
1/2 cup melted butter
1/2 cup unsifted flour
1 teaspoon baking powder
1/2 teaspoon salt
8 ounces diced chiles

For 3 round quiche dishes:

15 eggs
1 1/2 pints creamed cottage cheese
1 1/2 pounds Jack cheese with Jalapeno peppers
1/2 cup melted butter
3/4 cup unsifted flour
1 1/2 teaspoons baking powder
1/2 teaspoon salt
12 ounces diced chiles

Preheat oven to 350 degrees Fahrenheit.

Beat eggs and add all other ingredients. Bake in round buttered quiche dishes for 35 minutes until firm or knife comes out clean. Serve with salsa.

Optional: Mushrooms and spinach can be substituted for chiles.

Serves: 2 quiches - 16; 3 quiches - 24

Baked Eggs

10 eggs, beaten
2 cups melted butter
2 cups all-purpose flour
2 teaspoons salt
Pepper to taste
1 pint small curd cottage cheese
1 cup grated cheddar cheese
3 green onions, finely chopped (chives may be substituted)

Preheat oven to 325 degrees Fahrenheit.

Spray 9x13-inch baking dish with vegetable oil. In a large bowl combine the eggs, butter, flour, salt and pepper, stirring until well blended. Add the cottage cheese, cheddar cheese and chives. Pour into prepared baking dish. Bake for 35 to 45 minutes or until the eggs are firm and cooked through. Cut into individual pieces and serve immediately.

Note: Can be prepared the night before and baked in the morning. Remove from refrigerator 30 minutes before baking.

Serves: 6 to 8

Baked French Toast

A favorite at our Inns and so easy to do. Best of all, it can be set up the night before and just popped into the oven in the morning just before you're ready to sit down.

- 1 cup maple syrup
- 1 loaf French bread
- 3 eggs
- 3 egg whites
- 1 1/2 cups skim milk
- 2 teaspoons vanilla extract
- 3/4 teaspoon ground nutmeg

Lightly spray or wipe a large baking dish with vegetable oil. Pour the syrup into the dish. Slice the French bread into eight 2-inch thick slices and place them over the syrup.

In a separate bowl, combine the eggs, egg whites, milk, vanilla, and 1/4 teaspoon nutmeg, and beat until well mixed. Pour the egg mixture over the bread, pressing the bread down gently so it soaks up the batter. Cover and refrigerate overnight.

Preheat oven to 350 degrees Fahrenheit.

Remove the pan from the refrigerator and sprinkle the remaining 1/2 teaspoon nutmeg over the bread; bake for 40 to 45 minutes, or until golden brown. Serve with fresh fruit, if desired.

Serves: 8

Lemon Soufflé Pancakes

6 eggs, separated
2 cups small-curd cottage cheese
1/4 cup vegetable oil
2 tablespoons maple syrup or granulated sugar
1/2 teaspoon salt
4 teaspoons freshly squeezed lemon juice
4 teaspoons baking powder
1 cup unbleached all-purpose flour

Preheat a griddle or a large heavy skillet.

In a bowl, beat the egg whites until stiff but not dry. Reserve.

Combine the cottage cheese, egg yolks, oil, syrup, salt, lemon juice, baking powder, and flour in a food processor or blender and blend until smooth. Fold in the egg whites. Lightly oil the griddle, spoon on the batter, about 3 tablespoons for each pancake, and bake until the tops are bubbly. Turn and cook until bottoms are done. Serve hot with your favorite toppings.

Serves: 4-6

Persimmon Bread

Out by our pool, we have a very large, very beautiful old persimmon tree. During the summer and fall, we have Friday night wine tastings there for our guests with local winemaker friends. In the winter we pick the beautiful red orange fruit that looks like Christmas balls hanging in the tree and make Persimmon Pudding and Persimmon Bread. Both are favorites here at the inn.

    2 eggs
    3/4 cup sugar
    1/2 cup oil
    1 cup persimmon pulp
    1 teaspoon baking soda
    1 1/2 cups flour sifted
    1 teaspoon cinnamon
    1/2 teaspoon salt
    1/2 cup walnuts, chopped
    1/2 cup raisins (optional) chopped

Preheat oven to 325 degrees Fahrenheit. Blend eggs, sugar and oil together. Mix soda into pulp. Add to sugar mixture. Sift flour before measuring. Add cinnamon and salt to flour. Add coarsely chopped nuts to dry ingredients and fold into persimmon mixture. Pour into oiled 3x 4x 9-inch pan. Bake for 1 hour 15 minutes.

Yield: 1 loaf

Popovers

The secret to successful popovers is very hot popover pans and do not skimp on shortening or butter. For maximum puffiness, avoid over beating the batter or opening the oven door until the popovers are almost done. Serve piping hot with plenty of butter and jam or honey.

    4 eggs
    2 cups whole milk or half and half
    2 cups sifted unbleached all-purpose flour
    2 teaspoons granulated sugar
    1/4 teaspoon salt
    2 tablespoons butter, melted

Preheat oven to 450 degrees Fahrenheit.

Prepare popover pans or custard cups by placing 1/2 teaspoon of shortening into each cup and place into oven while preparing batter. Combine the eggs, milk, flour, sugar, and salt, and beat with a wire whisk or blender just enough to blend. Stir in the melted butter. Remove popover pans from the oven and fill cups about three-quarters full. Bake until golden brown and firm to the touch, about 35 minutes. When done, serve immediately.

Note: If you prefer drier interiors, remove the popovers from the pans or cups and replace them at an angle. Pierce each with a skewer, turn off the heat, and let them stand in the oven, with the door ajar, for about 8 minutes.

Yield: 8

Tomato Frittata

2 tablespoons unsalted butter
3 tablespoons light cream (or half and half)
 2 sliced tomatoes, sliced
1/2 teaspoon salt, or to taste
1/4 cup chopped fresh herbs
Freshly ground black pepper
8 eggs

Heat butter in 8-inch non-stick skillet over low heat. Add the sliced tomatoes and cook about 5 minutes on medium heat. Turn tomatoes.

In a bowl, beat the eggs. Add the herbs, light cream, cheese, salt and black pepper to taste.

Pour the egg mixture over the tomatoes. Turn heat to very low and cook the omelet until the eggs are set around the edges. Then gently lift edges of the omelet with a spatula and tilt the pan to let the uncooked egg run underneath. Continue cooking until the eggs have almost set on top. Place a plate over the top of the pan and invert, turning the frittata onto the plate. Add the remaining 1 tablespoon of butter and oil to the pan and slide the frittata back into the pan, cooked side up. Cook until the bottom is set, 2 to 3 minutes. Loosen the edges of the frittata with a spatula and slide it onto a plate.

Serves: 6

Secluded beneath towering redwoods in the charming hamlet of Occidental, the Inn at Occidental is centrally located to the spectacular vineyards and orchards of Sonoma wine country, the stunning beaches and cliffs of the Pacific Coast and the delightful, meandering Russian River.

Inn at Occidental

www.innatoccidental.com

800-522-6324 • 707-874-1047

3657 Church Street • P.O. Box 857 • Occidental, CA 95465-0857

Signature Recipe

Baked Praline French Toast

1 loaf French bread (13 to 16 ounces)
8 large eggs
2 cups half and half
1 cup milk
2 tablespoons granulated sugar
1 teaspoon vanilla extract
1/4 teaspoon cinnamon
1/4 teaspoon nutmeg
Dash salt

Slice bread into 20 slices, 1 inch thick. Arrange slices in a generously buttered 9x13-inch baking dish in 2 rows, overlapping slices. In a large bowl, combine eggs, half and half, milk and remaining ingredients. Pour mixture over the bread slices, making sure all are covered evenly. Spoon some of the mixture between the slices. Cover with foil and refrigerate overnight.

Preheat oven to 350 degrees Fahrenheit.

Spread Praline Topping evenly over the bread and bake for 40 minutes, until puffed and lightly golden. Serve with maple syrup if desired.

Serves: 10

Praline Topping

1/2 pound unsalted
   butter (2 sticks)
1 cup packed light brown sugar
1 cup chopped
   pecans
2 tablespoons light corn syrup
1/2 teaspoon cinnamon
1/2 teaspoon nutmeg

Combine all ingredients in a medium bowl and blend well.

Baked Lemon Eggs

1/2 cup heavy whipping cream
1 1/2 teaspoons finely grated lemon peel
1/2 cup grated Gouda cheese
8 eggs
2 tablespoons chopped fresh parsley
Salt and pepper to taste

Preheat oven to 350 degrees Fahrenheit.

Liberally butter four (12 to 14 ounce) baking dishes or ramekins. Pour 1 tablespoon cream into each baking dish. Sprinkle lemon zest equally into each dish. Sprinkle 2 tablespoons grated cheese over lemon and cream. Gently break 2 eggs into each dish. Add salt and pepper to taste. Pour 1 tablespoon cream over each dish. Scatter parsley garnish on top. Bake for 12 minutes or until eggs are just set.

Serves: 4

Buttermilk Waffles with Mixed Berry Sauce

2 cup unbleached all-purpose flour
1 1/2 teaspoons baking soda
1/2 teaspoon salt
1/4 teaspoon nutmeg
1 3/4 cups buttermilk
2 large eggs, separated
1 tablespoon sugar
6 tablespoons unsalted butter, melted
1 teaspoon vanilla extract

Stir together the dry ingredients. In another bowl, mix buttermilk, egg yolks, melted butter and vanilla. Stir wet ingredients gently into dry ingredients. Do not over mix. Beat the egg whites to stiff, glossy peaks, and then fold them gently into the batter.

Heat waffle iron and bake the waffles according to manufacturer's instructions.

Mixed Berry Sauce

3 cups fresh or frozen mixed
   berries
1/2 cup sugar
1/2 teaspoon ground cinnamon
1/4 teaspoon ground nutmeg
1 teaspoon grated lemon zest
2 tablespoons corn starch
1/4 cup cold water
Juice 1 lemon
1 teaspoon vanilla extract

In saucepan combine the berries, sugar, cinnamon, nutmeg and lemon zest. Simmer about five minutes, enough to soften berries. In a small bowl combine cornstarch and water, stirring to dissolve any lumps. Add cornstarch to berry mixture and stir over low heat until thickened, about 5 minutes. Remove from heat, stir in lemon juice and vanilla, and adjust sweetness if necessary.

Serves: 4

Lemon Ricotta Pancakes

1 1/2 cups all-purpose flour
2 tablespoons granulated sugar
1 teaspoon baking soda
1/2 teaspoon salt
1 1/2 cups buttermilk
2 large eggs, separated
1 tablespoon grated lemon peel
1/3 cup part skim ricotta cheese

In a large bowl mix flour, sugar, baking soda and salt. In a medium bowl whisk buttermilk, egg yolks, and lemon peel to blend. Stir buttermilk mixture into flour mixture just until evenly moistened. Gently stir in ricotta cheese.

In a separate bowl, beat egg whites until soft peaks form. Gently fold the whites in the batter just until incorporated.

Heat griddle on medium heat. Test temperature by spritzing water on griddle until water sizzles. Lightly film the griddle with butter or oil. Drop 1/4 cup batter onto griddle for each pancake. When bubbles on surface of pancake break, flip pancake. Cook another 1 1/2 to 2 minutes until done.

Serve hot with maple syrup or lemon curd.

Yield: 8 pancakes/4 servings

Orange Pancakes

1 1/2 cups all-purpose flour
1/2 teaspoon salt
1 teaspoon baking soda
1 tablespoon sugar
2 teaspoons baking powder
1 egg, separated
3/4 cup orange juice
3/4 cup buttermilk
5 tablespoons butter, melted

Whisk together the flour, sugar, salt, baking powder, and baking soda in a medium-sized bowl. Place the cooled melted butter and egg yolk in a small bowl and whisk to blend. Add the buttermilk and orange juice. Whisk thoroughly to combine. Pour the liquid ingredients into the dry ingredients and mix until combined. In a separate bowl, beat the egg white to stiff peaks. Fold into batter. Do not over mix. The batter should be quite thick and lumpy.

Spoon batter onto hot, greased griddle. When bubbles form on surface, flip pancakes. Cook until browned on both sides. Serve with Orange Syrup.

Orange Syrup

1/2 cup butter, melted
3 tablespoons cornstarch
2/3 cup granulated sugar
1 ounce orange zest
2 cups orange juice
1/4 cup pure maple syrup

Melt the butter with the cornstarch for 1 minute. Cool. Heat juice and add. Stir until thickened. Add sugar. Bring to boil, simmer for 5 minutes. Add maple syrup, and keep warm until ready to serve.

Yield: 8 pancakes/4 servings

Sonoma Strawberry Streusel Muffins

1 1/4 sticks (12 tablespoons) unsalted butter, melted
1 3/4 cups all-purpose flour
1 tablespoon baking powder
1 1/4 teaspoons cinnamon
1/4 teaspoon salt
1 teaspoon vanilla extract
2/3 cup granulated sugar
2/3 cup whole milk,
   room temperature
1 large egg
1 1/4 cups diced strawberries*
Streusel topping
   (recipe below)

Preheat oven to 400 degrees Fahrenheit.

Butter a standard muffin tin. In large bowl, whisk together flour, baking powder, cinnamon, and salt. In a separate bowl, whisk together butter, vanilla, sugar, milk, and egg. Fold butter mixture and the strawberries into flour mixture just until mixed. Do not overmix.

Spoon 1/4 cup batter into each prepared muffin cup. Gently press 2 tablespoons streusel on top. Bake 15 to 17 minutes until tops are golden. Cool in pan 15 minutes before transferring to wire rack.

Streusel Topping

2/3 cup all-purpose flour
2/3 cup confectioner's sugar
1/4 teaspoon cinnamon
Pinch salt
5 tablespoons unsalted butter, melted

Whisk dry ingredients together. Add melted butter and combine, using your fingers, until mixture is crumbly.

*Other fruit or berries may be substituted.

Yield: 1 dozen

Triple Chocolate Cookie

3 ounces unsweetened chocolate
7 tablespoons unsalted butter
1 1/2 cups semi-sweet chocolate chips
3 eggs
1 cup granulated sugar
1 teaspoon vanilla extract
1 tablespoon instant espresso powder
1/2 cup all-purpose flour
1/2 teaspoon baking powder
1/2 teaspoon salt
11/2 cups milk chocolate chips

Preheat oven to 350 degrees Fahrenheit.

Combine unsweetened chocolate, butter, and semi-sweet chocolate chips in the top of a doubleboiler, and melt over simmering water. Set aside to cool. Place eggs and sugar in bowl of mixer and whip 3 to 4 minutes, until lemony yellow and fluffy. Add vanilla and espresso powder. Slowly add melted chocolate mixture and beat until combined. Sift together the flour, baking powder and salt. Add dry ingredients to chocolate mixture and combine at low speed. Fold in milk chocolate chips.

Hold dough at room temperature for 30 minutes. Drop by teaspoons onto parchment-lined cookie sheet. Bake for 12 minutes.

Yield: 3 dozen

The Irish Rose is a wonderful Craftsman home located in the heart of Dry Creek Valley, near Healdsburg, Sonoma County.

Built in 1902, the inn has two guest rooms available which are named after the Proprietor's children Michael and Kimberly. Michael's room has a king-size bed and private bath with separate walk-in shower and spa tub. Kimberly's room has a queen-size bed and private bath with spa tub and overhead shower. Also available on the property to rent are "Chateau Margi," a one bedroom cottage with kitchen family room combo, and "First Crush," a two bedroom two bath cottage with fireplace and kitchen.

Irish Rose Inn

www.theirishroseinn.com
707-431-2801
3232 Dry Creek Road • Healdsburg, CA 95448

Signature Recipe

Hash Brown Quiche

 3 cups frozen loose-pack shredded hash browns, thawed
1/3 cup butter
1 cup fully cooked ham, diced
1 cup (4 ounces) shredded cheddar cheese
1/4 cup green pepper, diced
2 eggs
1/2 cup milk
1/2 teaspoon salt
1/4 teaspoon pepper

Preheat oven to 425 degrees Fahrenheit.

Press hash browns between paper towels to remove excess moisture. Press into the bottom and up the sides of a greased 9-inch pie plate. Bake for 25 minutes.

Reduce heat to 350 degrees Fahrenheit.

Combine the ham, cheese and green pepper: spoon over the crust. In a small bowl, beat eggs, milk, salt and pepper. Pour over all. Bake for 25 to 30 minutes or until a knife inserted near the center comes out clean. Allow to stand for 10 minutes before cutting.

Serves: 6

Asparagus and Egg Biscuit Bake

1 1/2 pounds of asparagus (or more) cut in 1-inch pieces
1 dozen hard-boiled eggs
2 cans of mushroom soup
1/2 soup can of milk
Grated cheese
2 refrigerated tubes of biscuits (10 each)

Preheat oven to 350 degrees Fahrenheit.

Cook asparagus pieces about 3 minutes in boiling water. Arrange cooked asparagus and sliced hard –boiled eggs in a large flat casserole dish. Top with grated cheese. Mix the soup and milk and pour over the eggs. Bake for 10 minutes. Top with biscuits and bake at 375 degrees for 10 minutes, or until the biscuits are brown.

Serves: 6

Goat Cheese Dip

1 cup olive oil
1/3 cup fresh basil, chopped
1/3 cup sun dried tomatoes,
 chopped
1/4 cup fresh parsley,
 chopped
1/4 teaspoon dried thyme
1/4 teaspoon hot pepper
 flakes
1/2 teaspoon dried rosemary
4 to 5 cloves of garlic, minced
2 large goat cheese logs
 (freeze slightly to slice, or
 just crumble)

Crumble or slice cheese into the bottom of a serving dish. Chop all other ingredients and combine in bowl. Pour over goat cheese. Marinate overnight (or at least a couple of hours) in the refrigerator.

Leave out at room temperature for at least 1 hour before serving.

Serve with sliced baguette or crackers.

Serves: 10

Pear Pie

2 ready-to-bake pie shells (leave out of refrigerator overnight)

Preheat oven to 425 degrees Fahrenheit.

Arrange crusts in two 10-inch tart pans and bake each for 10 minutes

> 6 pears, peeled and sliced
> 2/3 cup melted butter
> 1/3 cup sugar
> 2/3 cup flour
> 6 eggs
> 1 1/2 teaspoons almond flavoring

Preheat oven to 350 degrees Fahrenheit.

Arrange the pears in the partially baked pie shells. Mix the remaining ingredients and pour over the pears. Bake for about 35 minutes. Slice into small wedges, and sprinkle with powdered sugar.

Yield: 16 to 20

Sleepover Coffee Cake

2 cups flour
1 cup sugar
1 cup buttermilk
2/3 cup butter or margarine, softened
1/2 cup brown sugar
2 large eggs
2 tablespoons dry milk powder
1 tablespoon cinnamon
1 teaspoon baking soda
1 teaspoon baking powder
1/2 teaspoon salt

Topping:

1/2 cup brown sugar
1/2 cup chopped walnuts or pecans
1/2 teaspoon ground nutmeg
1/4 cup butter or margarine, melted (next day)

Grease and flour a 9x13-inch baking pan.

In large bowl of an electric mixer, combine all cake ingredients. Mix at low speed until well blended, about 4 minutes. Place in prepared pan. Mix dry topping ingredients together and sprinkle evenly over the batter. Refrigerate overnight.

The next morning preheat oven to 350 degrees Fahrenheit.

Melt butter and drizzle over cake. Bake for 30 minutes, until top is rich golden brown. Cool for 15 minutes and serve warm.

Serves: 8 to 10

Sophie Bean's Roasted Chicken

We live on a farm and Sophie Bean takes care of the chickens so we named this recipe for her.

    3 carrots, peeled and cut into 1-inch pieces
    3 ribs celery, peeled and cut into 1-inch pieces
    3 onions, peeled and cut into small chunks
    One 3 1/2 to 4-pound chicken
    1 1/2 tablespoons kosher salt
    2 teaspoons cracked black pepper
    1 lemon, halved
    2 fresh bay leaves
    6 cloves garlic, chopped
    4 sprigs rosemary, roughly chopped, plus 1 tablespoon for gravy
    2 tablespoons olive oil
    2 tablespoons unsalted butter
    1 cup chicken stock or broth
    2 tablespoons roasted garlic
    1 cup dry white wine

Preheat oven to 500 degrees Fahrenheit.

In a 9x13-inch roasting pan, add carrots, celery and onions. Season chicken both inside and out with kosher salt and white pepper. Squeeze lemon halves over chicken and place rinds and bay leaves inside the cavity. In small bowl, combine garlic, rosemary, olive oil and butter. Rub chicken both inside and out with garlic-rosemary blend and place in roasting pan.

Roast chicken for 40 to 50 minutes, or until juices run clear. To test, insert a thermometer in thickest part of leg. It should register an internal temperature of 160 degrees. Remove chicken from oven and allow to cool for 10 to 15 minutes before carving.

Pour or spoon excess fat from pan and return to heat. Whisk in chicken stock, roasted garlic, white wine and chopped rosemary, scraping up bits on bottom of pan. Bring to a boil and reduce to a simmer. Reduce gravy by half or until thickened.

Serve chicken with gravy on the side.

Servings: 6 to 8

Toasty Baked Oatmeal

2 cups regular rolled oats
1 1/2 teaspoons baking powder
1/2 teaspoon salt
1/3 cup chopped almonds
1/3 cup chopped dried apricots
1 firm ripe 8-ounce pear, rinsed, stemmed, cored, and chopped into 1/4-
  inch pieces
1 1/2 cups milk
2 large eggs
1/2 cup firmly packed brown sugar
3 tablespoons vegetable oil
1/2 teaspoon ground cinnamon

Preheat oven to 325 degrees Fahrenheit.

In large bowl, mix oats, baking powder, and salt. Stir in almonds, apricots, and pear.

In another bowl, whisk together the milk, eggs, brown sugar, oil, and cinnamon. Pour over the oat mixture and stir to combine.

Pour mixture into a buttered 8-inch square baking pan. Bake until liquid is absorbed and top is light golden, about 45 minutes. Spoon into bowls and serve warm.

Serves: 4

·Melitta Station Inn·
ENGLISH
Bed & Breakfast
Est. 1882

A charming Victorian village lodging-house was converted into a unique and intimate English style B&B by the English owners Tim and Jackie Thresh. Here they have brought inimitable hospitality to a location where the city meets the countryside;

they follow green practices, are solar powered and environmentally sensitive. Decorations in a cottage style with hand-crafted soft furnishings complement antiques collected by the owners. English afternoon tea with scones is served on genuine period English porcelain tea-services. The visitor can walk into Annadel State Park, and visit all Sonoma County wine appellations and even Napa Valley within 30 minutes. Owners: Jackie & Tim Thresh

"Real English hospitality in the heart of Sonoma Wine Country"

Melitta Station Inn

www.melittastationinn.com
707-538-7712 • 800-504-3099
5850 Melita Road • Santa Rosa CA 95409

Signature Recipe

Olde English Figgy Pudding

This early Victorian dish, which suits cold weather, can be found in Charles Dickens' stories, and is sung about in Christmas carols. "Bring us Figgy Pudding, Bring it right Now!..."

- 1/4 pound dried figs
- 1/4 pound pitted prunes
- 2 cups apple juice
- 4 cups breadcrumbs made by using up stale bread (not commercial variety)
- 4-ounce stick of butter, melted
- 2 cups half and half
- 3 eggs
- 1 cup dark brown sugar (preferably raw)
- 1 teaspoon apple pie spice
- 2 teaspoons cornstarch

Soak prunes and figs overnight in the apple juice.

Preheat oven to 375 degrees Fahrenheit.

Drain and chop the fruit. Reserve the liquid which will now be dark brown.

Mix all dry ingredients except cornstarch together with the melted butter. Beat eggs and cream together and add to dry mixture. Gently fold in the chopped fruit.

Grease a large round-bottom heatproof bowl with butter. Pour in the mixture and bake for 45 to 50 minutes until firm to the touch.

OR take 1 cup of the mixture and pour into a well-greased muffin tin or small bowl (as pictured) to make individual portions. Bake for 30 to 35 minutes.

While the pudding is cooking, place 1 cup of remaining fruit juices in small saucepan and add cornstarch, blend well and bring to a boil until clear. Add a little honey to sweeten to taste.

Cut large pudding into portions and serve (or individual puddings) with sliced fruit and sauce drizzled over one side.

This freezes well both cooked and uncooked.

Serves: 6

Asparagus Eggs Benedict

3 eggs plus 2 for poaching
1 English muffin opened "on the round"
1 cup half and half
1/2 cup condensed asparagus soup
6 to 8 asparagus spears
Seasoning to taste: salt, pepper and a pinch of mustard
2 slices of smoked salmon
Hollandaise sauce

Place half a muffin cut side up in a greased cocotte (heat-proof) dish.

Beat together eggs, half and half, soup and seasoning. Pour egg mixture over muffin half and let soak for about 30 minutes.

Preheat oven to 350 degrees Fahrenheit.

Trim off tough end of each asparagus stem. Cut a two-inch length off tip of each spear, and thinly slice the rest into rounds. Poach the asparagus pieces in a little water, with the tips on top of the rounds, for about 5 minutes. When cooked, reserve the tips, drain and add the rounds to the sauce around the muffin. Stir in gently to distribute.

Just before serving, poach the eggs to taste. Reheat the asparagus tips. Remove the cooked dish from the oven and garnish with asparagus spears, a poached egg, smoked salmon, and accompany with hollandaise.

Serves: 2

Caramel Oranges

Marinade (make weekly and store in refrigerator):

> I orange
> 1 cup sugar
> 1/2 cup orange juice

Peel orange with vegetable peeler and shred finely. Place in a small saucepan, cover with water. Simmer for 10 to 15 minutes until tender. Strain. Combine 1 cup of cooking liquid to 1 cup of sugar and boil until golden brown. CAREFULLY pour in orange juice, and leave to cool

Add the shredded peel and store in the refrigerator.

Oranges:

> 4 or 5 oranges

Peel and remove the skin and pith from the oranges using a serrated-edge knife so that there is no thin skin left on the orange segments underneath. Clean and remove any remaining pith between the segments using sharp scissors. Slice thinly across the orange to create rounds cut across the segments. Arrange five or six slices on individual plates layering in a circular fan. Pour caramel sauce over and let marinate for at least 4 hours.

Serves: 6

Cranberry Walnut Strata

7 eggs
6 ounces cream cheese
1 1/2 cups half and half cream
1/2 cup sugar
Grated rind of an orange
1/4 cup of orange juice
1 teaspoon vanilla essence
1/2 cup cranberries
1/3 cup chopped walnuts
Loaf of white sliced bread
1 teaspoon sugar + 1/2 teaspoon cinnamon

Grease and line an 8x6-inch ovenproof dish with the bread (crusts removed). Blend together eggs, cheese, cream, sugar, zest, orange juice, and vanilla. Sprinkle cranberries and walnuts over bread. Fill center with egg mixture. Cover top with slices of bread. Cover dish tightly with plastic wrap and refrigerate overnight

Preheat oven to 350 degrees Fahrenheit.

Remove plastic from dish and sprinkle top with sugar/cinnamon mixture. Bake uncovered for 40 minutes until golden brown. Serve with chicken-apple sausages and pureed carrots for color.

Serves: 6

Eggplant Stacks

1 one-pound eggplant
1 one-pound tube pre-cooked polenta
1 8-ounce onion, peeled and chopped
2 tablespoons of fresh herbs (basil,
   oregano and thyme work well)
1 14-ounce can tomatoes, drained
   (retain the juice) and chopped
Salt and pepper
1 1/2 cups of Mexican mix shredded
   cheese
Sprigs of fresh rosemary to garnish
2 slices of sprouted grain whole
   meal bread for Melba toast

Preheat oven to 425 degrees Fahrenheit.

Lightly coat 14x17-inch baking sheet with olive oil cooking spray.

Rinse eggplant, trim and discard both ends. Cut at an angle into slices about 1/2 inch thick. Cut polenta into the same number of slices, cutting at an angle as necessary so polenta matches size of eggplant slices. Arrange eggplant slices topped by polenta slice evenly on baking sheet in single layer. Lightly coat tops with cooking spray. Bake until eggplant is soft when pressed and polenta is heated through, about 20 to 25 minutes. Do not let slices brown.

In an 8 to 10-inch fry pan over medium heat, stir together onion and herbs, stirring occasionally until the onion is lightly browned, about 5 minutes. Add chopped tomatoes and 1/4 cup of juice and simmer uncovered until flavors blend, 5 to 10 minutes. Add salt and pepper to taste. Cover and keep warm until eggplant is ready.

When eggplant is soft, spoon onion-tomato mixture carefully on top of polenta to form mound. Return sheet to oven for 5 minutes. Next sprinkle 1/4 cup of cheese over each eggplant mound and return to oven for 2 minutes or until cheese melts. Garnish with fresh rosemary, and slice of Melba toast (see below)

Serves: 4 to 6

Melba toast:

While the stacks are baking, toast the wheat bread until brown. Carefully split each slice into two thin slices with a sharp serrated edge knife. Place the slices on a baking sheet and put in the same oven (at the same temperature as the stacks) for 5 minutes to dry and toast the moist side.

English Tea Scones

1 rounded teaspoon baking powder
2 cups self-rising flour
2 ounces salted butter
1/4 cup sugar
6 ounces (3/4 cup) milk

Preheat oven to 425 degrees Fahrenheit.

Rub butter into the flour and baking powder until you achieve a "crumb-like" texture. Add sugar. Bind together with milk and gently knead (lightly) into a dough. Roll out on floured surface until dough is 1-inch thick. Using a 2 1/2-inch to 3-inch pastry cutter, cut out 10 rounds. Knead and roll remaining dough to 1-inch for additional scones. Place each round on a greased baking sheet and bake on the top shelf of a hot oven for 12 to 15 minutes, checking after 10 minutes as the scones will burn easily. When tops are golden brown, remove from oven and allow to cool on wire rack.

Split each scone horizontally and serve with homemade strawberry jam or lemon curd and crème fraiche.

Note: Creme Fraiche is often the nearest available equivalent to "Cornish Clotted Cream" which you may find in your specialty deli.

Yield: 10

Swedish Egg Cake with Seasonal Fruits

10 ounces of any stale cake (provided it has no butter-cream or frosting and is not strong flavored)

7 ounces of cream cheese (must be Philadelphia brand)

2 ounces sugar

1 cup of half and half

4 eggs

1 teaspoon cinnamon

1 teaspoon vanilla extract

Blend together all ingredients except cake crumbs. Place cake crumbs in a mixing bowl and pour the blended mixture over the crumbs. Cover and refrigerate to soak overnight.

In the morning, preheat the oven to 375 degrees Fahrenheit.

Mash the soaked crumb mixture with a potato masher and pour into a really well-greased 10 -inch ceramic flan dish. Bake for 30 to 40 minutes until golden brown. Allow cake to cool slightly before cutting and serving.

Prepare fresh seasonal fruits according to availability and preference. Hint: use apple juice to avoid color deterioration in apple, pear, banana and other sensitive fruits.

Cut wedge-shaped portions of the cake and serve with a dusting of powdered sugar.

Garnish plates artistically with the fruits and a sprig of mint.

Serves: 6

This bed and breakfast retreat is set on a quiet, secluded hillside near Cloverdale, Geyserville and Healdsburg. Founded as a hunting retreat by railroad magnate Charles Crocker in the 1880s, the Crocker Ranch and its 1906 lodge and cabins offer 10 luxury guest rooms and suites, each with private bath and entry, gas fireplace, and air conditioning. Enjoy full breakfasts, house baked goods, in-room massage, swimming pool and plenty of space to relax. Just minutes from dozens of world-class wineries.

Old Crocker Inn

www.oldcrockerinn.com
707-894-4000 • 800-716-2007
1126 Old Crocker Inn Road • Cloverdale, CA 95425

Signature Recipe

Belgian Waffles with Fresh Berries

Light and crispy and the recipe is easy to double, triple and more.

- 3/4 cup all-purpose flour
- 1/8 cup flaxseed meal (optional)
- 1/4 cup corn or potato starch
- 1/2 teaspoon salt
- 1/2 teaspoon baking powder
- 1/4 teaspoon baking soda
- 3/4 cup buttermilk
- 1/2 cup milk
- 1/4 cup vegetable oil
- 1 large egg, separated
- 1 tablespoon sugar
- 1/2 teaspoon vanilla extract

Whisk together first six ingredients. In separate bowl, lightly beat egg yolk with fork, add milks and oil and whisk until combined. Beat egg white to almost soft peaks. Sprinkle in sugar and beat until peaks are firm. Beat in vanilla. Pour buttermilk mixture into dry ingredients and stir just until mixed. Lumps are okay – don't over mix. Let sit 10 to 15 minutes.

While batter is resting, plug in waffle maker. Spray or brush with oil (repeat for each batch).

Fold egg white mixture into batter just until blended. Don't beat.

Ladle batter over bottom of waffle maker and cook according to manufacturer's instructions. Ours takes about 5 minutes.

Serve with fresh berries, dusting of confectioner's sugar, and bacon with maple or berry syrup on the side. If not serving the waffles immediately, lay on racks in warm oven but don't stack or they will get too soft.

Variations: Add 1/2 cup mini chocolate chips or 2 teaspoons orange zest and 1/2 cup coarsely chopped dried cranberries or blueberries to batter.

Yield: Five 4 1/2-inch squares

Alexander Valley Eggs Benedict

Fresh eggs from a local farmer and the addition of fresh vegetables enhance this traditional breakfast dish.

Hollandaise Sauce

> 4 eggs yolks
> 1/2 pound (2 cubes) butter, melted and hot
> 1 tablespoon cream
> 1 tablespoon lemon juice, to taste
> Pinch cayenne pepper
> Pinch salt

In blender, mix eggs and cream until frothy. Slowly pour in 1/2 of the hot melted butter through top opening of blender (cover on to avoid splatter) and blend. Add lemon juice and blend. Add remaining butter and blend. Add pepper and salt and blend until thickens nicely. Taste and add more lemon juice if needed. Keep warm.

> 4 eggs
> 4 whole-wheat English muffins, split
> 1 large tomato
> 2 cups fresh spinach, chopped
> 4 slices Canadian bacon
> Paprika

Cut off the ends of the tomato and slice into four pieces. Sauté in skillet on both sides. Wilt spinach in tablespoon of water in skillet. Squeeze out excess water. Warm bacon in skillet. Poach eggs in egg poacher for 4 minutes or until whites set and yolks soft and jiggly. Toast muffins.

To serve, layer from bottom to top: half a muffin, spinach, tomato slice, other half of muffin, bacon, poached egg, Hollandaise sauce and sprinkling of paprika.

Serves: 4

Butternut Squash Cake

Squash cake? That skepticism is quickly dispelled with the first bite of this moist flavorful cake.

- 4 ounces (1/2 cup) unsalted butter, softened
- 3 cups all-purpose flour
- 1 1/2 cups white sugar
- 1/2 cup canola oil
- 2 large eggs
- 1 tablespoon distilled white vinegar
- 2 teaspoons vanilla extract
- 1 teaspoon baking soda
- 1 teaspoon salt
- 1/2 teaspoon ground ginger
- 1/4 teaspoon grated nutmeg
- 3/4 cup buttermilk
- 2 1/2 cups grated butternut squash (use large holes on box grater)

Preheat oven to 325 degrees Fahrenheit.

Butter and flour a Bundt pan. In large bowl with hand mixer or stand mixer with paddle attachment, beat butter and sugar on medium speed until well combined, about 1 minute. Add oil and beat until combined. Add eggs, one at a time, mixing well on low speed. Add vinegar and vanilla and mix again just until combined.

Whisk together flour, soda, salt and spices. Add half the flour mixture to batter, mixing on low speed just until combined. Add half the buttermilk and mix until combined. Repeat with remaining flour and buttermilk.

Stir squash into batter and place batter in prepared pan. Bake until cake tester comes out clean, about 1 hour.

Cool on wire rack for 30 minutes; then invert cake onto rack and remove the pan. Cool completely. Pour icing back and forth in thick ribbons on cooled cake.

ICING

- 2 1/4 cups confectioner's sugar
- 3 tablespoons buttermilk
- 1 teaspoon vanilla extract
- 1/4 teaspoon nutmeg
- 1/4 teaspoon salt

In medium bowl, sift sugar and whisk with buttermilk, vanilla, nutmeg, and salt until smooth. Add more buttermilk a few drops at a time until icing is pourable but still quite thick.

Cherry Pecan White Chocolate Scones

3 cups all-purpose flour
1/2 cup brown sugar
1 tablespoon baking powder
12 teaspoon baking soda
1/2 teaspoon salt
3/4 cup unsalted butter, cut into small pieces (handle as little as possible)
1/2 cup dried cherries or cranberries, chopped
1/2 cup pecans, chopped and toasted
1/2 cup white chocolate, chips or shaved from block
1/2 teaspoon vanilla extract
1 cup buttermilk

Preheat oven to 400 degrees Fahrenheit.

Cover cookie pans with parchment paper or silicone baking sheets.

Mix cherries, nuts, and chocolate in small bowl.

Place flour, sugar, baking powder, soda and salt in bowl of food processor. Pulse until mixed.

Add butter and pulse just until mixture resembles coarse cornmeal. Dump butter mixture into large bowl and stir in cherry mixture with fork. Combine vanilla and buttermilk and add to dry ingredients, stirring with fork just until moistened. Turn dough onto lightly floured surface and knead just until combined and smooth, 8 to 10 times. Shape into ball. If dough is sticky, dust hands with flour. Cut ball into four smaller balls. Press each into circle about 1/2-inch thick. Cut into wedges – whatever size you like – separate, and place on baking sheet. Bake until very lightly browned and firm enough to pick up, about 8 minutes depending on size and oven.

Note: The key to tender scones is very cold butter and as little handling as possible.

Yield: 18 to 24 depending on size

Poached Eggs and Sausage Patties on Polenta

Make sausage ahead of time for the flavors to blend.

Sausage Patties

1 pound ground pork or turkey
  (or mixture)
1/2 teaspoon dried cilantro or thyme
1/2 teaspoon cumin

1 teaspoon light brown sugar
1/4 teaspoon cayenne or more to taste
1/2 teaspoon salt
1/4 teaspoon pepper

Mix spices together and add to pork, combining well. Refrigerate overnight to blend flavors. When ready to use, divide into 10 balls and flatten into thin patties about 3 inches in diameter. Cook in hot skillet about 3 to 4 minutes on each side until golden brown. Don't overcook or they'll be rubbery. If not using all patties, freeze before cooking.

Salsa

1/8 cup mild roasted chipotle sauce
  (Arriba! brand is good) or to taste
6 Roma tomatoes, diced small

2 scallions, chopped small
1/4 cup flat-leaf parsley, chopped

Place all ingredients in saucepan and cook until vegetables are soft. Keep warm but don't allow to boil.

Polenta

1/2 cup polenta
2 1/4 cups chicken stock (homemade or use Better than Bouillon with water)
1/3 cup Gruyere or Parmesan cheese, grated

Bring liquid to boil and slowly stir in polenta. Cook and stir at reduced heat for 10 minutes. Remove from heat and stir in grated cheese. Keep warm and stir occasionally.

4 to 8 eggs   1 tablespoon vinegar

Poach eggs in egg poacher or in pot of boiling water with vinegar.

To serve, spoon about 1/4 cup polenta onto plate for 1-egg serving, top with sausage patty, poached egg, and several spoonsful of salsa. Double everything for 2-egg serving. Garnish with fresh cilantro and slice of orange, twisted.

Serves: 4 (2 eggs/person) more (if 1 egg)

Spinach Bacon and Mushroom Crepes

Crepes

1/2 cup cake flour, sifted
1 cup milk, room temperature
2 eggs, room temperature
Dash Worcestershire sauce

Pinch of salt
2 tablespoons butter, melted
and slightly cooled

Whisk eggs and milk together. Stir in sifted flour, salt and Worcestershire; add butter and stir well. Allow batter to sit an hour or so. Stir to recombine and add a little water if too thick. It should resemble heavy cream. Note: Batter can also be made in a blender. Place all ingredients in the blender and mix at high speed for about 10 seconds; scrape down sides and blend another 10 seconds.

For best results, use 9-inch crepe pan. Heat pan over medium-low heat, lightly brush bottom with butter, pour scant 1/4 cup batter into pan, immediately swirl to coat the pan, cook until top is dry, flip crepe and cook another 10 seconds. Layer with waxed paper to prevent them from sticking together. Can be made in advance and kept warm in oven.

Filling

6 slices of bacon
1/2 pound fresh mushrooms,
  sliced
1 bag of baby spinach or 3 cups
  chopped full-leaf
2 tablespoons butter
1/4 cup flour

1 cup milk
1 tablespoon fresh parsley, finely
  chopped (more if using for garnish)
2 tablespoons Parmesan, grated
Pepper to taste
Capers
Crème fraiche

Cook bacon until crispy, drain on paper towels, and crumble when cool. Sauté mushroom slices in 1 tablespoon of bacon drippings. In skillet, wilt spinach in 2 tablespoons of water, drain on paper towels. Melt butter in saucepan, whisk in flour, stirring constantly until smooth paste forms. Gradually stir in milk and continue stirring until thick gravy forms. Add bacon, mushrooms, spinach, parsley, cheese and pepper and cook over low heat until somewhat thick, about 10 minutes.

Spoon filling along center of open crepe, and roll up. Top with capers, crème fraiche and chopped parsley.

Serves: 4

Zucchini Muffins

Millet gives these muffins a satisfying crunch and the nickname *Birdseed Muffins*.

1 3/4 cups flour	2 eggs
1/2 teaspoon salt	1/2 cup canola oil
3/4 teaspoon baking soda	1 1/2 teaspoons vanilla extract
1/2 teaspoon baking powder	1 teaspoon grated lemon rind
1 1/2 teaspoons cinnamon	2 cups grated zucchini (squeeze gently in clean dish towel to reduce moisture)
1/2 teaspoon ground ginger	
1/2 teaspoon ground nutmeg	1/4 cup millet
2/3 cup white sugar	Pecan halves
1/2 cup brown sugar	

Preheat oven to 350 degrees Fahrenheit.

Grease 12-cup muffin pan. Whisk together flour, salt, baking soda, baking powder and spices.

Beat together brown and white sugars and eggs at medium speed for 2 minutes. Add oil, vanilla and lemon rind, and beat another minute.

Stir in zucchini and millet. Stir in flour mixture, combining everything but not over mixing.

Fill muffin cups 2/3 full and top each with a pecan half.

Bake about 15 minutes. Test with toothpick. Bake another minute or two until toothpick comes out clean. Let sit in pan about 5 minutes and then run a knife around edge and lift out gently.

Wonderful as is or with a local honey or house-made marmalade.

If not eating immediately, cool completely and store in zip lock bag in freezer. To serve, warm in 200-degree oven for 10 minutes.

*In the middle of nowhere ...
and at the center of everything!*

This Russian River bed and breakfast is a Victorian farmhouse dating back to the 1870's with four bedrooms, private baths and fireplaces. A hot tub nestled in the redwoods to soothe the soul sits on our wrap-around veranda. We offer gourmet breakfasts, wine and cheese, and after-dinner homemade sweets and tea.

Bob and Betsy's breakfasts are served with flair and are absolutely delicious with only the best ingredients and recipes that inspire guests to eat with delight. Wine tasting, hiking, canoeing and biking need a hearty morning meal like French toast with seasonal fruit flambé.

Santa Nella House Bed and Breakfast

www.santanellahouse.com
707-869-9488 • 877-869-9488
12130 Highway 116 • Guerneville, CA 95446

Signature Recipe

Bob's Famous French Toast
with Nectarine Flambé Syrup

1 loaf of sweet French bread, cut into 1-inch slices
6 to 8 eggs
8 ounces of milk
1 teaspoon vanilla
Pinch of salt

Place eggs, milk, vanilla and salt in mixing bowl and beat well. Place sliced bread in a 9x13-inch Pyrex baking dish and pour egg mixture over slices. Coat well and then turn bread slices over. Cover and refrigerate overnight.

Preheat oven to 400 degrees Fahrenheit.

Heat buttered griddle and brown bread slices on both sides. Wash baking dish and butter the bottom. Place the browned bread in the pan and bake for 20 minutes.

Nectarine Flambé Syrup:

3 to 4 ripe nectarines, sliced
1 cup strawberries, sliced
3/4 cup unsalted butter
1 cup brown sugar
1 1/2 ounces of dark rum
1/4 teaspoon cinnamon

Place nectarines and strawberries in a bowl. Sprinkle with cinnamon and set aside.

Melt butter in sauté pan. Add brown sugar and heat until mixture boils and starts to thicken. Stand back and add rum, tipping pan to start the flambé. Let the fire subside and then add fruit. Cook 4 more minutes and serve over baked French toast.

Serves: 6 to 8

Blackberry Coffee Cake

2 1/4 cups flour
1 cup sugar
3/4 cup butter
1 teaspoon sugar
1/2 teaspoon baking powder
1/2 teaspoon baking soda
1/4 teaspoon salt
3/4 cup sour cream
2 eggs
1 teaspoon vanilla
8 ounces cream cheese, softened
1 cup blackberry jelly
1/2 cup slivered almonds

Preheat oven to 350 degrees Fahrenheit.

Grease and flour 10-inch springform pan. In a bowl combine flour and 3/4 cup sugar; cut in butter to resemble coarse crumbs. Reserve 1 cup of this mixture. Press the remaining into the pan and up the sides about 2 inches. To the reserved mixture add cinnamon, baking powder, baking soda, salt, 1 egg and sour cream; blend well. In another mixing bowl combine cream cheese, remaining 1/4 cup sugar, vanilla and 1 egg until well blended. Warm the jam in a small bowl, in the microwave for 20 seconds to soften.

Spread the cream cheese mixture over crust, then a layer of jam, then the reserved mix, spreading to cover completely. Top off with slivered almonds. Bake for 1 hour, until the filling is set and golden brown. Let cool for 15 minutes before removing sides of pan and then another 1/2 hour before serving.

Serves: 8 to 10

Carrot Muffins

All our guests love these vegan muffins.

- 3/4 cup bran flour
- 1/4 cup wheat germ
- 1 tablespoon arrowroot
- 1 teaspoon baking powder
- 1 teaspoon baking soda
- 1/3 cup maple syrup
- 1 cup water
- 1/4 cup canola oil
- 2/3 cup grated carrot
- 1 teaspoon allspice
- 1/2 teaspoon cinnamon

Preheat oven to 375 degrees Fahrenheit.

Spray 12-cup muffin pan with cooking oil.

Combine all dry ingredients. Then combine all wet ingredients and add to dry mixture. Mix well. Pour into prepared muffin pan and bake for 25 to 30 minutes.

Glaze:

- 2/3 cup powdered sugar
- 3 tablespoons maple syrup
- 1/4 cup pumpkin seeds

Mix powdered sugar and maple syrup until smooth. Drizzle over muffins and top with pumpkin seeds.

Yield: 12

Cherry Squares

These cookies are perfect for the holidays.

> 1 1/4 cups flour
> 1/3 cup packed brown sugar
> 6 tablespoons butter
> 1/2 cup chopped pecans
> 2 eggs
> 1 cup packed brown sugar
> 2 tablespoons flour
> 1/2 teaspoon baking powder
> 1/8 teaspoon salt
> 1 cup flaked coconut
> 1/2 cup white chocolate chips
> 1/2 cup chopped canned cherries, not pie filling

Preheat oven 350 degrees Fahrenheit.

Stir together 1 1/4 cup flour, 1/3 cup brown sugar and cut in butter until pea-size pieces. Add chopped pecans. Press into 9x9-inch square pan and bake for 15 minutes.

In separate bowl beat eggs until light. Mix in 1 cup brown sugar, 2 tablespoons flour, baking powder and salt. Then add coconut, white chocolate, and cherries. Spread evenly over the baked crust. Bake another 25 minutes until set and browned.

Cool completely before cutting.

Yield: 16 large squares

Enchiladas Huevos

With the addition of backyard chickens, we were looking for ways to use our fresh eggs. Bob came up with this recipe for the eggs and his desire to spice things up in the morning for our guests.

- 1 8-ounce can enchilada sauce
- 2 tablespoons butter
- 12 eggs
- 6 ounces ricotta cheese
- 6 green onions, chopped
- 6 of your favorite flour tortillas
- 8 ounces grated cheddar cheese or half cheddar and half Monterey Jack
- 2 tablespoons fresh cilantro, chopped

Preheat oven to 350 degrees Fahrenheit.

Spray 16x10-inch baking pan. Coat bottom of pan with enchilada sauce. Melt butter in a 12-inch skillet. Blend eggs, ricotta and green onions and scramble in warmed skillet, stirring gently until eggs are creamy and set to desired consistency.

Pour most of the rest of the enchilada sauce in a dish. Dip a tortilla in the sauce and coat both sides. Lay the coated tortilla in the prepared baking pan and then place egg scramble down the middle of the tortilla (dividing the scramble evenly among the 6 tortillas). Roll up the tortilla so that the seam is resting on the bottom. Repeat with the rest of the tortillas, filling the baking dish. Spoon remaining sauce over the top and sprinkle with grated cheese. Bake for 10 minutes.

To serve, sprinkle chopped cilantro over each tortilla and provide condiments such as avocado, sour cream and salsa. Add hot links or chorizo on the side.

Serves: 6

Ricotta Pancakes *Lighter than Air*
with Blueberry Pomegranate Syrup

Pancakes

When Bob made these for his young children, he would tell them to eat them quickly or hold them down with their fork or they would simply float away.

> 3 eggs
> 1 teaspoon baking powder
> 1 pinch salt
> Zest of one lemon
> 1/2 pound whole-milk ricotta
> 2/3 cup whole milk
> 1/2 cup flour

Separate egg yolks from whites. In a stainless steel bowl, whip egg whites until they are stiff, and set them aside. In a separate bowl, mix the rest of the ingredients just until blended and fold in egg whites.

Heat an oiled griddle. Ladle one spoonful of batter onto the hot griddle and cook until bubbles appear on the surface of the pancake. Flip the pancake and continue cooking until the underside is golden brown. Serve immediately with blueberry-pomegranate syrup and melted butter.

Blueberry Pomegranate Syrup

> 1 1/2 cups sugar
> 1 teaspoon cornstarch
> 3/4 cup pomegranate juice
> 2 1/2 cups fresh blueberries

In a medium saucepan, add sugar and pomegranate juice. Over medium heat, stir mixture until sugar is dissolved. Add cornstarch to 1/2 cup of sugar syrup and whisk until smooth. Slowly stir back into saucepan. Turn heat to high and bring mixture to a boil, uncovered and without stirring, for 5 minutes. Let this "simple syrup" cool.

Puree 1 1/2 cups of the blueberries in a blender or food processor and pour into a mixing bowl. Add 1/2 cup of the simple syrup and mix well. Taste to determine if you need more syrup to sweeten it to your liking. Add remaining berries to syrup mixture and fold them in gently. Warm slightly before serving.

Serves: 6

Vegetable Frittata

2 tablespoons olive oil
1 medium zucchini, sliced into 1/2 inch rounds
1 medium onion, sliced
4 artichoke hearts, cut into quarters
1 cup mushrooms, sliced
8 eggs
1 cup shredded cheese, part cheddar, part Parmesan
Salt and pepper to taste
1/4 cup mint or basil, chopped
8 cherry tomatoes, cut in half

Start oven broiler.

In a 10-inch ovenproof sauté pan, warm olive oil. Add zucchini, onions, artichokes and mushrooms. Sauté until onions are translucent; season with salt and pepper. In a mixing bowl, beat eggs. Add cheese and chopped mint; mix well and pour over sautéed vegetables. Cook over medium heat until eggs start to set. Decorate with cut tomatoes and place pan under broiler for 5 minutes or until the eggs are completely set and top is browned. Cool at room temperature for 10 minutes before cutting.

For more than four guests you could make 2 sauté pans or use a 12-inch pan and double the recipe. We also recommend cooling completely and as done in the Enotacas in Venice or Florence, cut into smaller pieces and serve as an appetizer.

Serves: 4 to 8

The Gables Wine Country Inn is a beautifully restored 1877 Victorian mansion in the center of California's spectacular Sonoma Wine Country. The Inn sits on three lush green acres with magnificent vineyard and valley views. Each of the spacious guestrooms and the cottage has been furnished and decorated to reflect the historical detail found in only the most elegant Victorian mansions.

The Gables Wine Country Inn

www.thegablesinn.com
707-585-7777 • 800-422-5376
4257 Petaluma Hill Road • Santa Rosa, CA 95404

Signature Recipe

Pecan Crusted Caramel French Toast

A favorite every time we serve it!

    8 slices French bread, at least 1 inch thick
    1 cup light brown sugar
    1/2 cup butter
    2 tablespoons maple syrup
    1 cup pecans, chopped
    6 eggs
    1 1/2 cups half and half
    1 teaspoon vanilla

Grease 9x13-inch pan. Cook brown sugar, butter and syrup over low heat until bubbly, stirring frequently, about 5 minutes. Pour evenly into prepared pan. Sprinkle chopped pecans over top. Place bread slices on top of pecan caramel mixture. In blender, whip eggs, half and half and vanilla thoroughly and pour evenly over bread. Cover with foil "tent" which has been sprayed with Pam on the underside so the bread won't stick to the foil. Let stand at least one hour or make the night before and refrigerate. Remove from refrigerator at least 30 minutes before baking.

Preheat oven to 375 degrees Fahrenheit.

Bake covered for 45 minutes. Very carefully invert onto baking sheet and gently separate into pieces.

Note: I serve this with sausage, ham or bacon alongside to balance the sweetness but you may also serve topped with unsweetened whipped cream, crème fraiche, and fresh fruit.

Serves: 8

Baked Banana Crumble

Guests LOVE this! I make up several batches of the crumble mixture ahead of time and keep it on hand in a plastic bag in the refrigerator – makes this recipe quick and easy!

    4 ripe firm bananas, peeled
    3/4 cup orange juice
    1 teaspoon vanilla
    1/2 cup flour
    1/2 cup quick-cooking oats
    3/4 cup brown sugar
    1/2 teaspoon ground nutmeg
    1/2 teaspoon salt
    6 tablespoons cold butter

Preheat oven to 375 degrees Fahrenheit. Slice bananas lengthwise and place, cutsides up, in 4 greased oval ramekins or custard cups. In small bowl, combine orange juice and vanilla; drizzle over bananas. In large bowl, combine flour, oats, brown sugar, nutmeg and salt. Cut in butter until mixture resembles small peas. Evenly spoon crumble mixture over fruit. Bake 15 to 20 minutes. Serve warm with vanilla ice cream if desired.

Serves: 4

Berry Soup

We serve this when we want to upgrade from a "smoothie". The flavor is so rich and the presentation is beautiful!

3 cups frozen mixed berries, partially thawed
1/3 cup sugar
1/2 cup Sonoma sparkling wine
2 cups sour cream or combination of sour cream and yogurt
2 tablespoons orange liqueur (Grand Marnier is best) or a drop
    of orange oil
Orange juice to blend, if needed

Process in blender until smooth, add orange juice if needed. Serve in stemmed glasses, small soup bowls or sherbet dishes with a dollop of whipped cream. Garnish with mint or a fresh strawberry.

Variation: This recipe is also lovely made with fresh or frozen peaches.

Yield: 4 to 4 1/2 cups or 35 to 40 ounces

Egg Nests with Hollandaise

Not only is this fun and easy to prepare, it's delicious! We serve this with steamed asparagus on the side.

- 3 cups fresh spinach leaves
- 6 sheets filo dough
- 1/4 cup grated Parmesan cheese
- 6 large eggs
- Fresh ground pepper
- 1/4 cup finely chopped green onions, including tops
- 1 cup hollandaise sauce or any cheese sauce you prefer
- Paprika

Preheat oven to 350 degrees Fahrenheit.

Stack 1/2 cup spinach leaves and cut into thin slivers. Lay 1 filo sheet flat and spray with Pam Butter Flavor cooking spray. Cover remaining dough with plastic wrap to prevent drying. Lay another filo sheet onto the buttered layer and spray lightly. Cut stack into 6 equal squares and cover with plastic wrap. Repeat to make a total of 18 filo squares. Butter 6 alternate cups of muffin pan. Press 3 filo squares into each cup, overlapping, to line the cavity smoothly. Filo edges will extend above the rim. Sprinkle 2 teaspoons grated Parmesan into each filo nest and top with about 1 tablespoon of slivered spinach leaves. Break 1 egg into each nest and sprinkle eggs equally with green onion and freshly ground pepper. Bake until filo is golden and eggs are softly set when gently shaken, 18 to 20 minutes.

To serve, mound remaining spinach equally onto plates. Using a pastry knife, gently lift egg nest from baking cups and set 1 or 2 on each plate. Add hollandaise or cheese sauce to taste. Dust with paprika.

Serves: 3 to 6

Incredible Gooey Oatmeal Cranberry Chocolate Chip Cookies

2 cups flour
1 teaspoon baking soda
1 teaspoon salt
1 cup butter, softened
1 cup granulated sugar
1 cup packed brown sugar
2 teaspoons vanilla
2 eggs
2 cups chocolate chips
2 cups dried cranberries
2 cups quick oats

Preheat oven to 350 degrees Fahrenheit.

Combine flour, baking soda, and salt in a small bowl and set aside. Beat butter, sugar, and vanilla in a large bowl until creamy.

Add eggs one at a time, beating well after each addition. Gradually beat in flour mixture. Stir in chocolate chips, cranberries, and oats. Drop onto ungreased cookie sheet (I use a large ice cream scoop!) and bake for 15 to 20 minutes. Allow the cookies to cool slightly on the cookie sheet; then remove to a wire rack to cool completely.

Yield: 24 large cookies

White Chocolate Coconut Macadamia Cookies

2/3 cup butter
2/3 cup sugar
1/2 cup packed brown sugar
1 large egg
1 teaspoon vanilla
1 1/2 cups flour
9 ounces white chocolate, chopped into 1/2-inch pieces (or bag of white chocolate chips)
1 1/2 cups shredded coconut
1 (3 1/2 ounce) jar salted macadamia nuts, coarsely chopped

Preheat oven to 325 degrees Fahrenheit. Lightly grease a cookie sheet. In a large bowl, beat the butter, both sugars, egg, and vanilla with an electric mixer until fluffy. Add the flour and beat just until blended. Stir in the white chocolate, coconut, and nuts. Drop heaping tablespoonsful (I use a large ice cream scoop!) at least 2 inches apart, onto the cookie sheet. Bake 17 to 20 minutes or until edges of the cookies are lightly browned and tops look dry. Allow the cookies to cool slightly on the cookie sheet, then remove to a wire rack to cool completely. Store the cookies in an airtight container.

Yield: 24 large cookies

Wine and Cheese Omelet

This is a variation of a recipe I cut out of my hometown paper 30 years ago. Still haven't figured out why it's called an "omelet" but guests love the flavor and are always impressed by the way it looks fresh out of the oven.

16 eggs
3 1/4 cups half and half
1/2 cup Sonoma dry white wine
1 tablespoon German mustard
1/8 teaspoon ground red pepper
4 large whole spring onions,
   minced
1/4 teaspoon freshly ground pepper
1 large loaf of Artesian French
   bread (something similar to a
   Gruyere Olive Garlic Bread), cubed
6 tablespoons butter, melted
3/4 pound Swiss or Gruyere cheese,
   shredded
1/2 pound Monterey Jack cheese,
   shredded
1 1/2 cups diced baked ham
   (optional)
1 1/2 cups sour cream
1 cup freshly grated Parmesan cheese (or1/2 cup Parmesan and 1/2 cup Swiss or Gruyere)

Beat together eggs, half and half, wine, green onions, mustard, pepper and red pepper until foamy. Stir in bread, melted butter, cheeses and ham. Cover bowl with foil and refrigerate overnight. Remove from refrigerator 30 minutes before baking.

Preheat oven to 325 degrees Fahrenheit.

Butter two 9x13-inch baking dishes. Divide mixture between baking dishes and bake covered until set, about 1 hour. Uncover, spread with sour cream and sprinkle with the Parmesan cheese or combination Parmesan and Swiss or Gruyere. Bake uncovered until crusty and lightly browned, about 15 minutes.

Note: I like to make this dish using individual ramekins. Reduce the initial baking time to approximately 30 minutes and then spread with sour cream and cheese and return to oven for another 10 minutes.

Serves: 12

This classic French Colonial landmark manor house, built in 1880, sits on a knoll with an unspoiled view of Russian River valley vineyards ringed by redwood-forested mountains. All rooms have full private baths, period antiques unique to each room, and a host of thoughtful amenities. Full hot gourmet country breakfast and evening wine and cheese reception are included. Lovingly preserved and operated, The Raford Inn is a place of quiet beauty in the hills of southwestern Healdsburg Wine Country.

The Raford Inn

www.rafordinn.com
707-887-9573 • 800-887-9503
10630 Wohler Rd • Healdsburg, CA 95448

Signature Recipe

Stuffed French Toast

This is our favorite Sunday breakfast, served with chicken or turkey sausage, and a starter of Homemade Granola and Organic Vanilla Yogurt

- 4 croissants
- 6 slices whole wheat bread
- 14 eggs
- 1 1/2 cups of milk
- 1 tablespoon cognac (optional)
- 1 tablespoon vanilla
- 1 1/2 teaspoons baking powder
- Cinnamon (about 2 teaspoons for sprinkling) divided in half
- Brown sugar (about 1/4 cup for sprinkling) divided in half
- 2 ounces softened cream cheese
- 1 cup of frozen or fresh mixed berries
- 1 banana

Grease a 9x13-inch glass baking dish.

Mix vanilla and baking powder in small dish.

Gently pull the crusts off the wheat bread and lay the remaining bread on the bottom of the dish.

Spread cream cheese over bread by dropping small dollops evenly with a teaspoon. Sprinkle with brown sugar and cinnamon. Slice the banana into coin-shaped pieces and lay evenly atop the brown sugar. Scatter berries over bananas.

Slice each croissant open like a sandwich. Lay halves flat and cut into 3 wedges each. Lay the wedges face down on top of berries with golden side up, piecing them together like a mosaic. Gently press down the croissants.

Mix together eggs, milk, cognac, vanilla, and baking powder. Pour mixture over bread. Sprinkle remaining cinnamon and brown sugar on top and gently press mixture down again to ensure all of the bread is saturated. Cover with Pam-sprayed foil and refrigerate overnight.

Preheat oven to 325 degrees Fahrenheit.

Bake covered with foil for 75 minutes. Cut into six squares; then cut each square diagonally into triangles for an attractive presentation. Sprinkle with powdered sugar.

Serves: 12

Chili Cheese Puff

6 eggs
1/4 cup flour
1/2 teaspoon baking powder
6 ounces (3/4 cup) small curd cottage cheese
12 ounces (1 1/2 cups) finely shredded Mexican cheese (or shredded
  Cheddar/Monterey cheese mix)
Small jar diced pimentos
4-ounce can diced chilies
3 to 4 shots Tabasco or hot sauce
Salt and pepper to taste

Combine all ingredients and refrigerate overnight.

Preheat oven to 350 degrees Fahrenheit.

Bake in greased 9-inch pie plate for 50 to 60 minutes. Let sit 5 to 10 minutes before serving. Serve topped with sour cream, salsa and guacamole, or sliced avocado.

Serves: 6 (4 if you use 8-ounce individual ramekins)

Chocolate Espresso Raspberry Brownies

2 sticks (1 cup) butter
1 cup + 3/4 cup chocolate chips (keep divided)
3 ounces unsweetened chocolate
3 eggs
1 tablespoon instant coffee powder
1 tablespoon vanilla
1 1/2 cups sugar
1/2 cup + 1/4 cup flour (keep divided)
1 teaspoon baking powder
1/4 teaspoon salt
1 1/2 cups chopped pecans
Raspberry syrup and fresh raspberries

Preheat oven to 350 degrees Fahrenheit.

Grease and flour 11x7-inch baking dish.

In small saucepan melt 1 cup chocolate chips, butter and unsweetened chocolate. Remove from heat and let cool slightly. In small mixing bowl, combine pecans, 1/4 cup flour and 3/4 cup chocolate chips. In another small mixing bowl combine 1/2 cup flour, baking powder and salt.

In medium mixing bowl, combine eggs, sugar, coffee powder and vanilla. Add cooled chocolate mixture and stir well. Then add flour mixture to chocolate batter and stir well. Finally, add pecan mix to batter and stir well.

Pour into prepared dish and bake 20 minutes. Put foil tent loosely over top and bake for 15 more minutes or until toothpick inserted in center comes out mostly clean. These brownies are RICH and MOIST so toothpick may not ever look completely dry.

Let cool for 1 hour before cutting into 24 squares and then 48 triangles. Brush tops with raspberry syrup and top with a half raspberry.

Yield: 48

Garden Vegetable Quiche

1 9-inch un-cooked pie shell
1 tablespoon olive oil
1 small white onion, cut into thin wedges
1/2 bell pepper (any color), chopped
1 small zucchini, sliced
1 small yellow squash, or crookneck squash, sliced
3 large fresh Swiss chard leaves, chopped
5 large fresh basil leaves, chopped
1 medium tomato, cut into thin wedges
1 teaspoon garlic salt
1/4 teaspoon pepper
6 eggs
1 cup skim milk
1/2 cup grated Asiago cheese
1/4 cup parmesan cheese, grated

Preheat oven to 375 degrees Fahrenheit.

In a large skillet, sauté onion, bell pepper, zucchini and squash until tender (do not brown). Add Swiss chard and basil leaves and steam with the lid on until leaves and stems are tender, about 5 minutes.

While veggies cook, mix eggs, milk, cheese, garlic salt and pepper in a medium-size mixing bowl. When veggies are done, pour egg mixture into the pie crust and add steamed veggies. Top with the tomato wedges and sprinkle with parmesan cheese.

Bake 30 to 35 minutes until knife inserted near center comes out clean. Let stand 5 minutes before serving.

Note: Fontina, Gouda, Swiss or Gruyere are all fine substitutes for the Asiago, alone or blended.

Serves: 6

Healthy Harvest Granola

Delicious as a topping for fresh fruit or served with yogurt or a little milk.

- 3 cups old-fashioned rolled oats
- 1/2 cup shredded coconut
- 1/2 cup sunflower seeds
- 2/3 cup sliced almonds
- 2 tablespoon raw sesame seeds
- 1/2 cup hulled green pumpkin seeds
- 2 tablespoons oat bran
- 2 tablespoons wheat germ
- 1/4 cup butter
- 1/4 cup honey
- 1 cup mixed dried berries
- 1/2 cup dried bananas

Preheat oven to 325 degrees Fahrenheit.

In a large bowl stir together dry ingredients except berries and bananas.

In a small saucepan melt butter with honey over low heat, stirring constantly. Pour butter mixture over oat mixture and stir until combined well.

In a large jellyroll pan, sprayed with non-stick spray, spread granola evenly and bake in the middle of the oven until golden brown, about 15 minutes total. Stir halfway through the baking. Cool granola in pan on a rack and stir in dried fruits. Granola may be kept in an airtight container at cool room temperature for about 2 weeks.

Yield: 6 cups

Mediterranean Frittata

8 large eggs
1 cup chopped water packed artichoke hearts (1/2 of 14-ounce can)
1/4 cup sliced black olives
1/4 teaspoon each salt and pepper
1/2 cup crumbled feta cheese
3 tablespoon sun-dried tomato pesto
1/2 cup bruschetta topping,* for garnish

Preheat oven to 350 degrees Fahrenheit.

Grease a 9-inch pie plate.

Beat eggs with fork and pour into prepared pie plate. Sprinkle artichoke hearts, olives, and feta cheese on eggs, gently stirring in. Dollop the pesto over the top of the eggs.

Bake for 45 minutes, until eggs are set.

Serve with fresh tomato/basil bruschetta topping.

Serves: 6

*Bruschetta topping is a mixture of fresh garlic, tomato, and basil (also sold in refrigerated or canned versions).

Orange Toasted Almond Scones

2 cups all-purpose
  flour
1/3 cup sugar
2 teaspoons baking
  powder
1/4 teaspoon salt
1/2 cup butter,
  chilled
2 eggs
1/4 cup orange juice
1 teaspoon vanilla
  extract
1 teaspoon grated
  orange peel
1/4 cup + 1 tablespoon toasted almonds, divided

Glaze

1 egg white mixed with 1/2 teaspoon water

Preheat oven to 400 degrees Fahrenheit.

In a large bowl, stir together flour, sugar, baking powder. Cut the butter into 1/2-inch cubes and distribute them over the flour mixture. With a pastry blender or 2 knives used like scissors, cut in the butter until the mix resembles coarse crumbs.

In a small bowl, stir together eggs, orange juice, vanilla, and grated orange peel.

Add the egg mixture to the flour mixture and stir to combine. Fold in the toasted almonds.

With heavily floured hands, form the dough into a ball and place it on a lightly floured piece of parchment paper. Roll the dough into an 8-inch diameter circle. Lightly dust the top with flour, and cut into 8 slices.

Carefully place slices onto a greased baking sheet. Brush the tops with the glaze and sprinkle with toasted almond slivers. Bake for 20 to 25 minutes until golden brown.

Serves: 8

Vintage Towers is a 1901 Queen Anne Victorian mansion, located in the small Sonoma Wine Country town of Cloverdale. The Inn has seven guestrooms, three of which are tower suites with sitting areas located in the Inn's uniquely shaped towers. We offer upscale eco-friendly lodging, including period antiques, feather beds, luxury linens and amenities, private baths with claw-foot soaking tubs, satellite TV, wireless internet access, customized concierge service and gourmet breakfasts. Just one block from downtown, the Inn offers easy access to restaurants, shops and local events in the town plaza.

Vintage Towers Bed & Breakfast Inn

www.vintagetowers.com
888-886-9377 • (707) 894-4535
302 North Main Street • Cloverdale, CA 95425

Signature Recipe

Artichoke Basil Frittata

2 tablespoons olive oil

1 small yellow or white onion, chopped

14-ounce can artichoke hearts/quarters in water, drained on paper towels, coarsely chopped

7 large eggs

1/4 cup sour cream or yogurt

Dash cayenne pepper

Dash ground nutmeg

Dash white pepper

1/2 teaspoon kosher or sea salt

5 large basil leaves

1/4 cup grated cheese, cheddar or Monterey jack, or a combination of the two

Preheat oven to 375 degrees Fahrenheit.

In large non-stick skillet, sauté onion and artichokes in olive oil over medium heat until lightly browned, about 10 minutes. Set aside pan to cool. Place next 7 ingredients in food processor or blender and process until smooth. When onions and artichokes have cooled until warm (not hot) stir in egg mixture and grated cheese. Grease 9-inch glass or heavy metal pie pan with shortening or butter. Pour in egg mixture and distribute evenly in pan. Bake 40 minutes until frittata is puffy, lightly browned and set in the center, rotating pan at 20 minutes. Cool slightly and cut into 6 to 8 wedges.

Serves: 6 to 8

Crunchy Almond French Toast

6 slices "French Toast" bread or "Texas Toast" bread
6 eggs
1 1/2 cups
 half and half
Dash cinnamon
Dash nutmeg
1 teaspoon
 vanilla extract
2 cups Almond
 Special K
 cereal
1 cup sliced
 almonds
Waxed paper
Butter
Cooking spray
Powdered sugar, orange wedges, sliced almonds for garnish
Syrups of choice for serving

Preheat oven to 375 degrees.

Place bread slices in 2 to 3- inch deep cake pan or casserole dish. Place next 5 ingredients in blender and blend until smooth. Pour over bread slices and let soak at least 15 minutes, turning at least once until almost all the liquid is absorbed. Cut bread in half diagonally into triangles. Pulse Special K cereal and sliced almonds in food processor until coarsely ground into large crumbs. Pour some ground cereal and almonds onto a sheet of waxed paper. Place piece of saturated bread on top of crumbs and pour more crumbs on top of bread. Pick up edges of waxed paper and gently move around until all sides of bread are coated. Place coated bread on cookie sheet to dry. Repeat process until all bread pieces are coated with crumb mixture. Melt about 2 tablespoons of butter in large frying pan over medium heat until bubbling. Sauté bread slices about 3 minutes on each side until brown and crispy. Place browned bread on cookie sheet coated with cooking spray. When all slices are browned, bake about 15 minutes until puffed and sizzling. Serve immediately, garnished with powdered sugar, orange slices and sliced almonds and hot syrups on the side.

Serves: 6

Orange Cherry Scones

3 cups all-purpose flour
1/4 teaspoon salt
1/3 cup white sugar
2 1/2 teaspoons baking powder
1/2 teaspoon baking soda
Zest of one lemon
Zest of one orange
1 1/2 sticks unsalted butter
3/4 cup milk
1/4 cup whipping cream
Juice of 1 lemon
1 cup dried cherries, cranberries or raisins
Raw sugar
1/2 teaspoon cinnamon

Preheat oven to 400 degrees.

Put all dry ingredients up through orange zest in food processor bowl and process until thoroughly mixed and zest is very fine. Add butter (in 1/2 stick chunks) and pulse until mixture resembles large crumbs. Dump in bowl and add dried fruit. Mix milk, cream and lemon juice in small container and dump into dry ingredients. Mix until barely moistened - don't overwork dough! Lightly dust large piece of parchment paper on cookie sheet with flour. Place dough on parchment and pat into a 1-inch thick circle about 12" in diameter using hands, and flour as needed. Dip long knife in flour and score into 16 pieces - cutting first into 8 wedges and then cutting each wedge into 2 pieces on diagonal. Sprinkle lightly with raw sugar and cinnamon. Bake approximately 22 minutes until lightly browned and toothpick stuck in center comes out dry. Slide parchment and scones onto rack to cool and cut with knife or cleaver when cooled.

Yield: 16

Pumpkin Pecan Zucchini Bread

3 cups all-purpose flour
1/2 teaspoon salt
1/2 teaspoon baking powder
1 teaspoon baking soda
1/2 teaspoon pumpkin pie spice
1/4 teaspoon ground cloves
1 teaspoon cinnamon
1/2 teaspoon ground nutmeg
3 large eggs
1 cup unsalted butter, melted
1 tablespoon vanilla extract
1 cup canned pumpkin
1 cup sugar
1 cup brown sugar, packed
1 cup chopped pecans
1 3/4 cups grated zucchini, drained and set on on paper towels to dry

Preheat oven to 350 degrees Fahrenheit.

Grease and flour two 9x5-inch or 8x4-inch loaf pans.

Whisk flour, salt, baking powder, baking soda, and all spices together in a bowl.

Mix eggs, butter, vanilla, pumpkin and sugars in a blender until creamy.

Add liquid mixture to dry ingredients in bowl and stir until just blended. Stir in zucchini and pecans.

Pour into prepared loaf pans and bake for about 60 minutes until tester inserted in center comes out clean. Cool in pan on rack for 20 minutes. Remove bread from pans and completely cool on rack.

Yield: 12 to 14 slices per loaf

Shirred Eggs

8 large eggs
Soft butter
4 tablespoons heavy cream
1/2 cup grated Parmesan cheese
1/2 cup grated cheddar cheese
Chives or scallions
Salt, pepper, paprika

Preheat oven to 375 degrees Fahrenheit.

Set eggs and butter out to warm up for at least an hour. Coat inside of four 6 to 8-ounce ovenproof ramekins with soft butter. Pour 1 tablespoon of heavy cream in each ramekin. Break two eggs gently in center of each dish. Sprinkle each with salt, pepper and finely chopped chives or scallions. Top with grated Parmesan and cheddar. Sprinkle lightly with paprika. Place ramekins in rimmed baking pan and bake about 21 minutes until almost set and tops are starting to brown. Serve with ham and buttermilk biscuits.

Serves: 4

Skillet Double Corn Bread with Honey Butter

1 1/4 cups all-purpose flour
3/4 cup yellow cornmeal
2 tablespoons white sugar
1 tablespoon baking powder
1/2 teaspoon salt
1/2 teaspoon freshly ground pepper
1 cup milk
1/4 cup vegetable oil
1 egg
1 15 1/4-ounce can whole-kernel corn, drained
Paprika

Preheat oven to 400 degrees Fahrenheit.

Coat a 9- or 10-inch cast iron skillet with nonstick vegetable spray. Place in oven for 5 minutes to preheat.

In large bowl, combine all dry ingredients with whisk. Add all liquid ingredients to bowl and stir just until combined. Stir in corn - don't overwork the dough. Spoon into preheated skillet and smooth with rubber spatula. Sprinkle with paprika.

Bake 25 minutes at 400 degrees until lightly browned and firm to touch. Let cool slightly, and then cut into 8 to 10 wedges and serve with honey butter (see recipe below).

Honey Butter

1 stick unsalted butter - best quality available
Honey

Bring butter to room temperature for at least half an hour. Place in bowl and drizzle with honey until top and sides are covered. Stir vigorously with fork until blended. Form into a ball and chill in refrigerator until set, 30 to 60 minutes.

Serves: 8 to 10

Spanish Soufflé

8 large eggs
2 cups heavy or whipping cream
1/2 teaspoon salt
1/2 teaspoon pepper
1/2 cup grated cheddar or jack cheese, or a combination
1/2 cup canned mild green chiles, drained in a sieve
Cooking spray
Fresh salsas, optional

Preheat oven to 350 degrees Fahrenheit.

Place eggs, cream, salt and pepper in blender and let sit at room temperature at least an hour to warm slightly. Spray eight 6–8-ounce ovenproof ramekins well with cooking spray until all sides and bottom are coated. Sprinkle approximately 1 tablespoon cheese and 1 tablespoon chilies in the bottom of each ramekin. Mix ingredients in blender on high until frothy. Pour into prepared ramekins. Bake for 40 minutes until puffy and lightly browned on top, changing racks and rotating after 20 minutes. Serve immediately with salsas of choice.

Serves: 8

We dreamed of owning a vineyard and making wine since we first met in 1983. It took us a decade before we planted our first vine, and then another six years before we found a magnificent vineyard just outside the charming village of Healdsburg. Along the way we learned a lot! Most importantly, that wine is a source of endless discovery and rich friendships.

Amista means "making friends". Our family-run, artisan winery showcases the beautiful fruit and friendly spirit of Sonoma's Dry Creek Valley. Our goal is to produce delicious wines that pair well with food and friends. Come visit our tasting barn, enjoy our wines and picnic in the heart of our vineyards surrounded by fabulous Dry Creek Valley views.

Vicky and Michael Farrow, Proprietors

Amista Vineyards
www.amistavineyards.com
www.facebook.com/amistavineyards
707-431-9200
3320 Dry Creek Road • Healdsburg, CA 95448

Amista Syrah Braised Short Ribs

A very tender bite-size beef rib in a rich and hearty French-inspired beef and red wine sauce. Serve alone or over garlic mashed potatoes. Pour a glass of Amista Syrah and enjoy!

2 pounds beef short ribs, cut to serving size
4 cups beef or vegetable stock
4 cups Amista Vineyards Syrah
1/4 cup olive oil
1/2 cup diced carrot
1/2 cup diced celery
1 whole sweet onion, diced
2 tablespoons tomato paste
1 teaspoon dry thyme
4 bay leaves
4 tablespoons flour
2 tablespoons butter
Salt and pepper to taste

Preheat oven to 250 degrees Fahrenheit.

Brown the short ribs in olive oil. Set aside. Sauté diced vegetables and thyme until golden. Stir in tomato paste. Add short ribs. Cover with wine and stock. Bake covered for 6 to 8 hours (until tender). Remove the short ribs (gently). Discard the bay leaves.

Optional: strain the juice from the ribs to remove the herbs and vegetables for a clearer sauce. Combine and whisk the flour and butter. Stir into juice from the ribs. Cook until thickened (about 3 to 5 minutes). Return ribs to pan; heat through and serve.

Serves 8

Suggested Pairing **Amista Syrah, Morningsong Vineyards, Dry Creek Valley (current vintage)**

Anaba

Anaba – named after the anabatic winds that enhance the quality of our vineyards – is a family-owned producer of small-lot Rhône and Burgundian grape varieties. Winemaker Jennifer Marion believes the art of winemaking finds its soul in the vineyard and produces our elegant wines from some of the best fruit in Sonoma County including our Carneros Estate 'J McK' Vineyard. Anaba is committed to all aspects of environmentally responsible winemaking and Anaba's wind turbine is the first in Northern California to generate power for a winery.

Anaba…elegant, classic wines borne by the wind.

Anaba Wines
www.anabawines.com
877-990-4188
60 Bonneau Road • Sonoma, CA 95476

Grilled Pork Tenderloin with Pinot Mustard Sauce

2 cups Pinot Noir
1 cup veal stock
2 tablespoons whole grain mustard
3 pork tenderloins, approximately 12 ounces each
Salt and pepper

To make the sauce, place wine in a small saucepan and reduce by half over high heat, about 10 minutes. Add stock and continue reducing the mixture by about 1/3, about 8 minutes more. Whisk in the mustard.

Preheat the broiler or oil the grill rack. Rub the tenderloins with salt and pepper. Grill the meat about 4 inches from heat about 12 minutes per side until just slightly pink inside. Allow to rest 5 minutes before slicing 1/4 inches thick. Serve with sauce.

Serves: 4 to 6

Suggested Pairing

**Anaba's
'J McK' Vineyard
Carneros Pinot Noir**

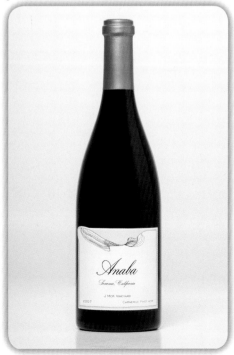

Applewood Restaurant
www.applewoodinn.com
800-555-8509
13555 Highway 116 • Guerneville, CA 95446

"Northern California's Applewood Inn offers world-class fine dining in a delightfully upscale restaurant."

This Sonoma/Russian River Restaurant is highly regarded for its exquisite cuisine, soothing atmosphere, polished guest services, and mellow earthy ambiance. The cozy restaurant was built to recall a French barn, yet gives one the feeling of being at a fine Italian villa. The restaurant is part of Applewood Inn, a Sonoma Bed and Breakfast boutique hotel. Both the inn and the restaurant have been touted by over 40 newspapers, magazines and public television shows. In the words of *Food & Wine Magazine: "Applewood Inn & Restaurant is an oasis of luxe!"*

Fine Cuisine among the redwoods: Set your GPS for this backwoods dinner destination. It's actually not hard to find, just over the river from the town of Guerneville, but it feels off the map, tucked into the secluded and peaceful Applewood Inn. The upstairs dining room makes a romantic venue, with cozy fireplaces and a solarium overlooking a trickling fountain and courtyard below.

Executive Chef: Bruce Frieseke, Sommelier: Christopher Jhones

Applewood Crab Cioppino

1/2 cup olive oil
1 red bell pepper, very small dice
1 Serrano chili, seeds removed, small dice
1 large onion, small dice
8 large garlic cloves- sliced thinly crosswise
1/2 teaspoon crushed red pepper flakes
1 carrot, small dice
2 stalks celery, small dice
1 bulb fennel, sliced vertically in 1/4 inch slices, and blanched in boiling water
2 large bay leaves
2 tablespoons tomato paste
1 cup white vermouth
One 28-ounce can peeled tomatoes, finely chopped, juice saved
Salt and pepper

4 cups fish stock or clam juice (we use crab stock)
1 bunch fresh basil, leaves picked off stems
1 bunch fresh flat-leaf parsley, leaves picked and finely chopped with basil
2 cooked Dungeness crabs, cleaned and quartered
1 dozen clams, rinsed and well cleaned (littlenecks are a nice size for stew)
1 pound mussels, rinsed, beard removed
1 pound any white fish cut in 1-inch cubes (halibut and rock cod are good)
1 pound large shrimp, shelled and deveined
1 pound sea scallops
1/2 pound calamari, bodies cut into rings, tentacles left whole

Pour olive oil into large stainless steel stock pot over medium heat. Add the peppers, onions, garlic, pepper flakes, carrot and celery, and cook, stirring occasionally for about 15 minutes, until softened and golden, With a wooden spoon, stir in the tomato paste so that it sticks briefly to the bottom of the pan. Deglaze with the vermouth and cook until reduced by half. Add chopped tomatoes (with their juice) and the bay leaves. Bring to a simmer and cook for about 5 minutes before adding stock or clam juice. Season stew with salt and pepper. Simmer again until broth thickens slightly, about 20 to 30 minutes.

About 20 minutes before serving, add crab, clams and chopped herbs to the pot. Adjust heat to resume a good simmer while you add cold fish and shellfish. When clams begin to open, about 5 minutes, add mussels, fish and scallops. When mussels begin to open, add shrimp and calamari, and cook about 3 minutes. Stew is ready when shrimp is tender and lightly cooked, calamari tentacles are umbrella-shaped, and all clams and mussels are open. (Discard any that aren't.) Divide crab and fish into serving bowls and ladle the soup. Serve with grilled rustic bread.

Serves: 4

Suggested Pairing **Saphire Hill Pinot Noir Russian River Valley 2008**

ARISTA

Arista Winery was founded by the McWilliams family in 2002 with a mission to create the most elegant expression of Russian River Valley Pinot Noir. We are committed to sustainable farming practices and sustainable business practices. We work closely with local growers who share our dedication to sustainability in their vineyards. We do not attempt to manipulate our vineyard sites but instead strive to preserve each vineyard's natural qualities.

We believe that wines made in the vineyard are well-behaved in the cellar. We coax them along with minimal intervention and gentle handling. Produced in small lots, Arista's wines have deep, rich flavors that reflect the unique sites from which they are sourced.

In addition to our wines, we pride ourselves on having created a true destination experience for our visitors. A breathtaking setting of Japanese water gardens, mountain and vineyard vistas, combined with an inviting tasting room, offers guests a welcoming environment that encourages picnic lunches and leisurely days spent on the estate.

Arista Winery
www.aristawinery.com
707-473-0606
7015 Westside Road • Healdsburg, CA 95448

Arista di maiale
Roast Loin of Pork
with Rosemary

4 to 5 pound loin
of pork, bone in
3 tablespoons
rosemary,
crushed
6 cloves garlic,
crushed
1 medium
onion, chopped
coarsely
1/4 cup olive oil
Salt and pepper
to taste

Preheat oven to 350 degrees Fahrenheit.

Have butcher either remove chine bone of pork roast, or break it to make carving easier. Remove most of excess fat from loin. With very sharp knife, make about a dozen small slits of various depths in loin – shallow to very deep.

Mix crushed rosemary and garlic together, with a little salt and pepper. The moisture of the fresh garlic should hold spices together. If not, add touch of olive oil. Place small amount of mixture into slits cut in loin. Use tip of finger to push to bottom of slit.

Heat butter in shallow roasting pan in preheated oven. Sprinkle onion over melted butter. Place pork loin directly on top of onion. Do not use a rack. Drizzle small amount of olive oil over loin. Roast uncovered for about 2 to 2 1/2 hours, or until thermometer registers 170 degrees Fahrenheit.

Serves: 12

Suggested Pairing **Longbow Pinot Noir, Russian River Valley**

BARTHOLOMEW PARK WINERY

Bartholomew Park Winery is a Sonoma Valley jewel that offers visitors one-of-a-kind access to one of the valley's most beautiful and historical winery settings. Enjoy hand-crafted wines produced with our 100% certified organic fruit, a picturesque private park, and gracious old world hospitality.   As a visitor to the winery, you are welcome to an atmosphere rich in natural beauty, site reflective wine character and an extensive and colorful history.

Bartholomew Park Winery
www.bartpark.com
707-935-9511
1000 Vineyard Lane • Sonoma, CA 95476

Finger Lickin' Spareribs

6 pounds country-style spareribs
1/2 cup sherry
1/2 cup water

Sauce

1 teaspoon salt
1/8 teaspoon pepper
1/4 lemon, sliced thin
1/2 cup onion, chopped finely
1 teaspoon chili powder
1 teaspoon celery seed
1 1/4 cup vinegar
1 1/4 cup Worcestershire sauce
1 six-ounce can tomato paste
3/4 cup brown sugar
1 cup water

In large frying pan, brown spareribs. Then add sherry and water and cover. Cook on low heat for one hour. Let spareribs cool in liquid long enough so you can skim off the fat. Remove spareribs and drain.

In another pan, combine all sauce ingredients and cook for one hour.

Preheat oven to 300 degrees Fahrenheit.

After spareribs have drained, lay in large shallow casserole or roaster. Cover with the sauce and bake for one hour.

Serves: 4

Suggested Pairing

**Bartholomew Park
Zinfandel, Estate Vineyard**

Nestled in the heart of the famed Russian River Valley, Benovia Winery produces iconic Pinot Noir, Chardonnay and Zinfandel wines with passion. After coaxing the very best fruit from its three estate vineyards – including the historic Cohn Vineyard – as well as grapes from select quality growers, Benovia handcrafts its traditional and modern style wines with a light touch. Owners Joe Anderson and Mary Dewane, Winemaker/ Co-owner Mike Sullivan, and General Manager Bob Mosby, lead the entire Benovia family in bottling the genuineness of a time and place that will always be the perfect complement to every gourmet meal.

EST. 2005

BENOVIA.

Winery

Benovia Winery
www.BenoviaWinery.com
707-526-4441
3339 Hartman Road • Santa Rosa, CA 95401

Dungeness Crab Cakes

Mike Matson, Executive Chef at Vintage Valley Catering, Healdsburg, California.

Often served at Benovia Winery events, this one is a real crowd pleaser!

        2 pounds lump Dungeness crab meat
        1/2 cup red bell pepper, diced
        1/2 cup red onion, diced
        1/4 cup green onions, sliced
        3 whole eggs
        1 cup toasted Japanese bread crumbs (Panko)
        4 tablespoons Dijon mustard
        2 tablespoons lemon juice
        1 tablespoon Thai chili paste
        1/4 cup peanut oil
        2 tablespoons butter

Preheat sauté pan with oil and butter. Mix remaining ingredients and form cakes into 4-ounce portions. Cook in oil and butter until golden brown. Serve with mixed greens and side of Aioli.

Serves: 8

Suggested Pairing

**Benovia Winery
"La Pommeraie"
Russian River Valley
Chardonnay**

We create handcrafted Bertapelle Cellars wines from our own estate vineyard and hand selected vineyards that meet our high standards of farming excellence. Fruit selection is paramount to our high quality wines. Our vineyards represent the Russian River and Dry Creek appellations where the fruit characteristics are developed from the rocky, but rich soils, the varied  hills and benches formed by the river, and the warm days and cool nights that are influenced by the summer fog coming up the Russian River Valley from the Pacific Ocean. Our limited production quantity allows our owners and winemaker to follow the wine making process carefully, with great attention to detail, in an artisan style. Producing only 500 cases per year, we sell directly to consumers via our web site, plus a few select restaurants and wine shops. We welcome you to explore the exciting grape to glass experience that is Bertapelle Cellars.

Bertapelle Cellars
www.bertapellecellars.com
707-433-5900
1160 Felta Road • Healdsburg, CA 95448

Duck Leg Confit

3 tablespoons kosher salt
4 cloves garlic, smashed
1 shallot, peeled and sliced
6 sprigs thyme
Coarsely ground black pepper
4 duck legs with thighs
1 cup olive oil

Sprinkle 1 tablespoon of salt in the bottom of a dish or plastic container large enough to hold the duck pieces in a single layer. Evenly scatter half the garlic, shallots, and thyme in the container. Arrange the duck, skin-side up, over the salt mixture, then sprinkle with the remaining salt, garlic, shallots, and thyme and a little pepper. Cover and refrigerate for 1 to 2 days.

Preheat the oven to 235 degrees Fahrenheit.

Brush most of the salt and seasonings off the duck. Arrange the duck pieces in a single snug layer in large baking pan, meaty side down. Pour olive oil over duck (duck pieces should be half covered by oil) and place confit in the oven. Cook confit at slow simmer for 1 1/2 hours. Turn duck legs over and continue cooking for another 1 1/2 hours, until duck is tender and can be easily pulled from the bone. Increase oven heat to 400 degrees Fahrenheit for about 20 minutes until the duck skin is nice and crisp.

Remove confit from the oven and serve over risotto or mashed potatoes and top with your favorite wild berry sauce, if desired.

Serves: 4

Suggested
Pairing

Bertapelle Cellars
Petite Sirah

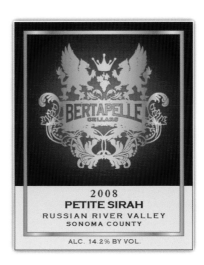

CAHILL
WINERY

Cahill Winery is located in Green Valley near Graton, California in the Russian River Appellation on Sonoma's West County Regional Trail. The winery was founded in July 2005 when Cahill acquired an existing kosher winery in the heart of apple country. The kosher winery production facility was replaced with traditional wine making practices and equipment to make aperitifs, ports and fine wines with future plans to make specialty grappas and apple brandies using locally grown, sustainable fruit products. Don Payne brings his expertise as a distiller and wine maker to create unique products. The winery staff and Payne family create a visitor friendly environment and welcome you to come enjoy our winery.

Cahill Winery
www.cahillwinery.com
707-823-1335
4950 Ross Road • Sebastopol, CA 95472

Ceviche with a Mojito

Ceviche

> 1 pound fresh halibut
> 1 green onion
> 6 limes
> 1/2 cup diced red bell pepper
> Salt and pepper
> 1/4 cup cilantro
> 1 jalapeño

Arrange the halibut in a deep dish and cover with lime juice. Refrigerate for about 6 hours. Turn once while chilling. Drain and reserve the juice. Break the fish up into small pieces.

Combine all the ingredients and add the reserved lime juice.

Serves: 6

Suggested Pairing **Cahill Winery's 24 Degrees Mojito**

Mojito

> Mint sprig
> 1 1/2 ounces 24 Degrees*
> 1 ounce simple syrup
> 3/4 ounce lime juice
> 2 ounces soda water
> Lime wedge

Serves: 1

*24 Degrees is produced at Cahill. They start with 100 percent California Chardonnay and run it through a traditional, artisan-quality pot still. The resulting high-proof alcohol then is blended to 48-proof, 24 percent alcohol. The final product, 24 Degrees, is clear and colorless and drinks very much like vodka or white tequila, but with a softer kick. It is completely dry, which sets it apart from other wine-based, fortified beverages like port, sherry or Madeira that are sweet and intended to be consumed as is.

Camellia Cellars

www.camelliacellars.com
707-433-1290
57 Front Street • Healdsburg, CA 95448

Camellia Cellars has been making award-winning wines from Sonoma County's Dry Creek Valley since 1983. The winery was bonded in 1997 following years of home winemaking by owner Ray Lewand, daughter Chris Lewand and partner Bruce Snyder. It produces small lots of vineyard-designated zinfandel, sangiovese, cabernet sauvignon and Diamo Grazie, a proprietary blend made in a super Tuscan style.

Pumpkin Ravioli
with Walnut Sauce

Walnut Sauce
- 3/4 cup shelled walnuts
- 1/4 cup pignoli nuts (pine nuts)
- 1/2 teaspoon marjoram
- 3 tablespoons olive oil
- 1/2 cup ricotta
- Dash of nutmeg
- Salt and freshly ground pepper
- 1/2 cup heavy cream

In a wooden bowl, mash walnuts and pignoli until they have a grainy consistency. Add all remaining ingredients except cream. Can be made ahead to this point. Set aside.

Medium white sauce
- 2 tablespoons butter
- 2 tablespoons flour
- 1 cup milk
- Salt and freshly ground pepper.
- Dash of nutmeg

Heat butter, and as soon as it bubbles, add flour. Stir with a whisk until blended.

In a separate pan bring milk to a boil. Add to flour and butter, whisking quickly until smooth. Stir and cook over low heat for about 10 minutes.

Combine walnut mixture with white sauce and use extra cream to bring it to the consistency you want (or use drained cooking water from the ravioli to thin if needed). Taste and correct seasonings. Yield: 3 cups

Pumpkin ravioli

Buy or make your own pumpkin ravioli and cook as directed.

Pour sauce over ravioli and gently stir to coat.

Serves: 6 to 8

Suggested Pairing **Camellia Cellars Diamo Grazie, Dry Creek Valley**

Charles Creek Vineyard

www.charlescreek.com
707-935-3848
483 First Street West • Sonoma, CA 95476

Founded in 2002 by Bill and Gerry Brinton, Charles Creek Vineyard produces award-winning Chardonnays, Merlot and Cabernet Sauvignon, plus small lots

of Malbec, Tempranillo and Pinot Grigio. The grapes are sourced from some of the best known vineyards in the Sonoma and Napa Valleys, including the Sangiacomo, Hyde, Stagecoach and Schaefer Vineyards. The wines are available for sampling and sale in the Charles Creek Vineyard Tasting Room and Gallery on the Plaza in Sonoma.

Lemon Chicken

A family favorite! This is delicious with green beans and garlic mashed potatoes.

- 6 chicken
  breast halves
- 4 lemons
- 1/2 cup flour
- 1/2 teaspoon salt
- 1/4 teaspoon
  pepper
- 2 tablespoons
  olive oil
- 2 tablespoons
  brown sugar
- 1/2 can
  chicken broth

Preheat oven to 350 degrees Fahrenheit. Rinse and dry chicken breasts. Grate the rind from two lemons, yellow part only. Squeeze juice from two lemons into flat dish. Mix flour with the salt and pepper.

Dip chicken breasts into lemon juice and then into flour mixture, and sauté in batches in olive oil until nicely browned. Place browned pieces in single layer in a baking dish. Sprinkle grated lemon rind and brown sugar on top of chicken breasts. Thinly slice remaining two lemons and place slices on top of chicken. Pour chicken broth into bottom of dish along with any of lemon juice left from earlier step. Use a little more broth if you wish.

Cover with aluminum foil and take for one hour.

When you remove the foil, the most wonderful aroma greets you.

Serves: 6

Suggested Pairing **Charles Creek Las Patolitas Chardonnay**

CHATEAU ST JEAN.
SONOMA

Only the finest! Sonoma County with its remarkable breadth of superior growing regions is Chateau St. Jean's home. Founded in 1973, we have long been recognized as the leader of vineyard designated wines. Winemaker Margo Van Staaveren has over 30 years of winemaking experience and is an artisan Winemaker who prizes the rich, intense flavors of grapes grown in these superior vineyards. The winery is known for its superlative Reserve Wines and its Cinq Cépages Cabernet Sauvignon, a Bordeaux blend, named Wine of the Year in 1999 by the Wine Spectator Magazine.

Our Mediterranean Gardens are widely considered the most beautiful in all of Sonoma County. This elegant landscape with an abundance of exotic trees and flowers combined with numerous water features is the perfect backdrop

to enjoy a fabulous picnic while tasting world-class wines in a gracious environment.

Chateau St. Jean's Tasting Rooms are open daily from 10:00 a.m. to 5:00 p.m.

Chateau St. Jean
www.chateaustjean.com
707-833-4134
8555 Sonoma Highway • Kenwood, CA 95452

Crab Soufflé

1/2 cup onion, minced
1/2 cup of garlic grapeseed oil
1/2 cup flour, sifted
2 cups of milk, scalded
1 teaspoon white pepper
2 teaspoons Dijon mustard
Tabasco to taste
8 egg yolks
2 cups of Crab Cake Mix (without celery, panko, and eggs)
8 egg whites
1 teaspoon of cream of tartar
Salt
Grated parmesan for dusting cups

Preheat oven to 350 degrees Fahrenheit.

Spray soufflé cups or ramekins generously and dust with the parmesan. Sweat onions in oil in covered pan until translucent. Add flour and cook several minutes to make roux. Pour in milk, salt and pepper slowly. Cook, stirring continuously until mixture becomes thick. Spread out in a hotel pan (stainless steam table pan) to cool. Whip egg whites until frothy. Add tartar and whip to stiff peaks, do not over whip. Fold crab mixture into roux mixture, check for seasoning (Tabasco, white pepper, mustard powder). Fold in whites. Scoop into soufflé cups or ramekins, bake for 15 minutes, then check and bake until done, about 15 to 20 minutes longer.

Serves: 4

Suggested Pairing

Chateau St. Jean Chardonnay-Robert Young Vineyard

Costeaux French Bakery

www.costeaux.com
707-433-1913
417 Healdsburg Avenue • Healdsburg, CA 95448

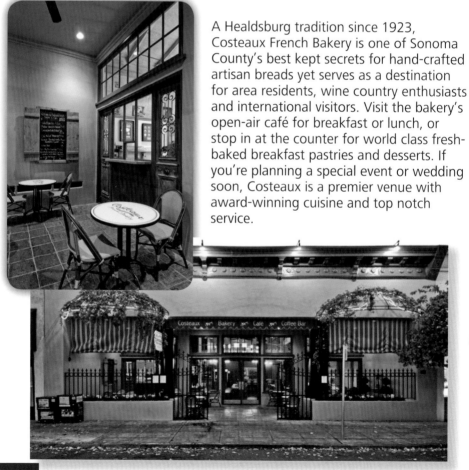

A Healdsburg tradition since 1923, Costeaux French Bakery is one of Sonoma County's best kept secrets for hand-crafted artisan breads yet serves as a destination for area residents, wine country enthusiasts and international visitors. Visit the bakery's open-air café for breakfast or lunch, or stop in at the counter for world class fresh-baked breakfast pastries and desserts. If you're planning a special event or wedding soon, Costeaux is a premier venue with award-winning cuisine and top notch service.

Costeaux French Bakery

Country Mustard Potato Salad

5 pounds potatoes
3 red onions, slice, then quarter slices
1/2 bunch parsley, chopped
3/4 cup sweet pickle relish
1/2 cup capers
1/2 cup whole grain mustard
2 cups house vinaigrette
Salt and pepper

Slice potatoes and cook in salted boiling water until tender but firm, about 5 to 8 minutes. When cool, add onion, parsley, relish and capers. Combine mustard and vinaigrette and add to potato mixture. Salt and pepper to taste.

House Vinaigrette Dressing

2 teaspoons each of fresh tarragon, basil, oregano and parsley
4 cloves garlic
1/4 cup shallots, peeled
1/4 cup Dijon mustard
2 teaspoons sugar
1 cup olive oil
1 cup red wine vinegar
2 cups vegetable oil
Salt and pepper

Chop fresh herbs in food processor. Add garlic, shallots, Dijon mustard, sugar, vinegar and blend well. SLOWLY add the oils to the mixture while blending in food processor. Add salt and pepper to taste.

Serves: 8 to 10

Suggested Pairing
Pedroncelli Sauvignon Blanc

DUTTON ESTATE
WINERY

Sebastopol
VINEYARDS
& WINERY CORP

Dutton Estate Winery specializes in single vineyard, Point Noirs, Chardonnays, Sauvignon Blancs, and Syrahs. Both Joe and Tracy Dutton have deep roots in farming and in the town of Sebastopol. Their goal is to produce the highest quality single vineyard wines from the Russian River appellation. Dutton Estate Winery has a warm friendly atmosphere that reflects the owners welcoming attitude.

We are open daily from 10-5. We offer several different flights including a cheese and wine pairing.

Dutton Estate Winery
Sebastopol Vineyards & Winery Corp
www.duttonestate.com
707-829-9463
8757 Green Valley Road • Sebastopol, CA 95472

Scallop and Orzo Salad with Tomatoes and Basil

1 pound petite sea scallops
1 pound dry orzo pasta
1/2 red bell pepper, minced
1/2 yellow bell pepper, minced
1/2 cup fresh basil leaves
2 medium tomatoes or cherry tomatoes, diced
2 tablespoons flour
1/4 cup olive oil for searing

Prepare herb and citrus dressing. Cook orzo in salted boiling water according to taste and drain. While still warm, toss with enough herb and citrus dressing to coat the grains well. Put to one side. Rinse scallops and pat dry with paper towels. Salt, pepper, and toss them with a few tablespoons of flour in a plastic bag. Heat olive oil in a frying pan and quickly sear scallops. Remove from pan, and allow to cool if you wish. Stir into the pasta, along with chopped or torn basil, diced fresh tomato and minced red and yellow peppers. Taste and add additional dressing, fresh ground pepper and salt, as needed.

Serve warm or cool.

Herb and Citrus Dressing

1/3 cup lemon juice (or lemon/lime combination)
1/3 cup orange juice (or orange/grapefruit combination)
2 teaspoons sugar
1 tablespoon Dijon mustard
3 cloves garlic crushed
1 teaspoon kosher salt
1/2 cup sweet herbs (such as parsley, coriander, basil) freshly minced
2/3 cup olive oil (or lemon olive oil)

Combine all but the oil and shake to mix well. Then add oil and shake well.

Serves: 6

Suggested Pairing **Dutton Estate's Kylies Sauvignon Blanc**

Family Wineries of Dry Creek

**Collier Falls Vineyards,
Dashe Cellars,
Forth Vineyards,
Lago di Merlo
Vineyards,
Mietz Cellars
and
Philip Staley Vineyards**

Family Wineries of Kenwood

**Cass Wines,
Collier Falls Vineyards,
David Noyes Wines,
Macrae Family
Vineyards,
SL Cellars,
Tres Hermanas
and
Wine Tree Farms**

Our tasting rooms offer a unique experience with multiple wineries in each location, emphasizing a wide range of areas, varietals and blends. An opportunity to taste small producers' wines in two convenient locations, both in the middle of wine country in Dry Creek and Sonoma Valleys. Better still join our wine clubs and receive reciprocal discounts from all of our wineries in either location. Come join the fun staff who will provide you a memorable highlight of your visit to Sonoma Wine Country.

FAMILY
WINERIES
DRY CREEK VALLEY
· KENWOOD ·

**www.familywines.com
888-433-6555
4791 Dry Creek Road • Healdsburg, CA 95448
9380 Sonoma Hwy • Kenwood, CA 95452**

Minestrone

2 cups dried beans (a variety of types)
1/2 pound summer squash (one whole, remainder chopped into small
    pieces)
2 potatoes (one whole, one chopped into small pieces)
2 carrots, chopped
3 celery stalks and tops chopped
1/2 small cabbage, leaves broken by hand.
3 celery stalks including tops, chopped
1 tablespoon olive oil
2 onions, finely chopped
3 slices bacon cut into pieces
Salt and pepper to taste
4 tablespoons Italian parsley,
    finely chopped
2 cloves garlic, crushed
Pinch of fresh marjoram
1 can skinless tomatoes (28 oz)
Cooked pasta (any bite-size
    variety)
1/4 cup basil, finely chopped
2 tablespoons parmesan cheese, grated

In a large bowl, place rinsed beans in six cups cold water and soak overnight. Reserve water.

In a large stockpot, cook beans slowly in reserved water for 1 to 1 1/2 hours. Cook squash, potatoes, carrots, celery, cabbage and parsley in separate stockpot, using ample water over medium/medium high heat for 30 minutes.

Heat olive oil in large sauté pan. Over medium heat, sauté onion and bacon to golden brown, add salt and pepper. Add chopped parsley, garlic, marjoram and tomatoes. Simmer for 10 to 15 minutes.

When vegetables are cooked, add to bean mixture along with water. Remove whole potato and whole squash, mash with spoon into tomato mixture. Add tomato mixture to boiling beans and vegetables.

Just before serving add cooked pasta, basil and parmesan. Total cooking time is approximate 4 to 5 hours (on a woodstove). Use fresh beans and vegetables when available in season.

Serves: 12

Suggested Pairing **Any hearty Red Varietal or Blend**

Freestone

Freestone Vineyards

www.freestonevineyards.com
707-874-1010
12747 El Camino Bodega • Freestone, CA 95472

Freestone Vineyards is location in the hamlet of Freestone bordering the Russian River on the Sonoma Coast. Freestone Vineyards specializes in world class Pinot Noir and Chardonnay. The Freestone wines are as much a revelation of its terroir as an expression of the grapes themselves. Each sip reveals not only the character of the varietal but also the flavors and aromas of the earth that nurtured it.

Ingeniously designed as a graceful continuation of the landscape, the Freestone winery is situated in the midst of the vineyards. Taking advantage of the building's three stories, the force of gravity is harnessed to transport wine from fermenters to barrels. The subterranean level is an ideal cellar environment where temperature and humidity are controlled naturally with minimal energy requirements.

The Freestone Vineyards Guest Center is ideally located to introduce visitors to Freestone Vineyards and the Freestone Community. The Guest Center provides a warm and welcoming venue for wine tasting and sales.

Pan-Seared Magret Duck Breasts

with Balsamic Blackberry Reduction

Balsamic Reduction

2 teaspoons extra virgin olive oil
2 teaspoons shallots, minced
1/2 teaspoon garlic, minced
1/2 cup dried blackberries (or dried cherries or blueberries)
1/2 cup balsamic vinegar
1 1/2 cups chicken sauce
2 teaspoons fresh sage leaves, chopped
1 tablespoon cold butter
Salt and pepper

Add olive oil to a 1-quart saucepan, set on medium-high heat. Once the oil is hot, add the shallots, garlic and dried blackberries and cook about 1 minute. Add the balsamic vinegar, cooking until the vinegar is almost completely reduced, about 2 to 3 minutes. Add the chicken stock and sage leaves and bring to a boil, then reduce the heat and simmer for 15 minutes. Once the sauce has cooked, swirl in small pieces of the butter until incorporated, off the heat. Season with salt and pepper to taste.

Duck Breast

2 Magret duck breast halves, 12 to 16 ounces each*
1 1/2 teaspoon kosher salt
1 teaspoon black pepper, freshly ground

Preheat the oven to 400 degrees Fahrenheit.

Score duck breasts on the fatty side, cutting about 1/8-inch into the skin in a cross hatch pattern. Heat oven-proof 12-inch sauté pan over medium-low heat. Season duck breasts on both sides with salt and pepper and place skin side down in hot skillet. Cook until skin is crispy, about 10 to 12 minutes. Pour off fat from pan. Turn breasts over and place in hot oven for 10 minutes. Remove from the oven and allow to rest for 3 to 4 minutes, then slice each breast into 12 slices. Drizzle with balsamic reduction.

* Smaller Muscovy duck breasts can be substituted.

Serves: 4

Suggested Pairing   **Freestone Pinot Noir**

Family owned and operated since 1979, our unique subterranean winery is nestled deep into a hill atop the Dry Creek Valley. Jay and Barbara Fritz purchased this pristine property in 1970 and turned the 115-acre parcel into a highly respected Estate Winery. Today our credo is to approach winemaking as an art form. Art, in its truest sense, inspires a shift in consciousness. Our mission is to create wines of genuine artistry, capable of transforming the way we think about the potential of Sonoma County's premier appellations.

Tasting Room open daily. 10:30am to 4:30pm
Tours by appointment only Saturdays and Sundays.
Picnic facilities with beautiful views available.

Fritz Underground Winery
www.fritzwinery.com
707-894-3389 • 800-418-WINE
24691 Dutcher Creek Road • Cloverdale, CA 95424

Beef Bourguignon
with Fritz Pinot Noir

Adapted by Natalia Fritz from Ina Garten, *Barefoot Contessa.*

1 tablespoon good olive oil
8 ounces dry cured center cut
applewood smoked bacon, diced
2 1/2 pounds beef chuck, cut into
1-inch cubes
Kosher salt
Black pepper, freshly ground
1 pound carrots, sliced diagonally
into 1-inch chunks
2 yellow onions, sliced
2 teaspoons chopped garlic
1/2 cup cognac
1 entire bottle of Fritz Pinot Noir

1 can beef broth
1 tablespoon tomato paste
1 teaspoon fresh thyme leaves
4 tablespoons unsalted butter at room
temperature, divided
3 tablespoons all-purpose flour
1 pound frozen whole onions
1 pound fresh mushrooms, stemmed,
caps thickly sliced
Fresh sour dough bread, thickly sliced,
toasted or grilled, rubbed with garlic
clove
1/2 cup chopped fresh parsley

Preheat oven to 250 degrees Fahrenheit.

Heat olive oil in large Dutch oven. Add bacon, cook over medium heat for 10 minutes, stirring occasionally until lightly browned. Remove and drain. Dry beef, sprinkle with salt and pepper, sear in single layer in hot oil for 3 to 5 minutes, browning all sides. Continue searing remaining beef.

Toss carrots and onions, 1 tablespoon of salt and 2 teaspoons of pepper in pan fat and cook for 10 to 15 minutes, stirring occasionally, until onions are lightly browned. Add garlic and cook for 1 more minute. Add cognac, stand back and ignite to burn off alcohol.

Put meat and bacon back in pot with juices. Add wine plus enough beef broth to almost cover meat. Add tomato paste and thyme. Bring to simmer, cover pot with tight-fitting lid and place in oven for about 1 1/4 hours or until meat and vegetables are very tender when pierced with a fork.

Combine 2 tablespoons of butter and flour with fork; stir into stew. Add frozen onions. Sauté mushrooms in 2 tablespoons of butter for 10 minutes until lightly browned; add to stew. Bring stew to boil on top of stove, lower heat, simmer for 15 minutes. Season to taste.

To serve, spoon stew over slice of bread; sprinkle with parsley.

Serves: 6

 Suggested Pairing **Fritz Dry Creek Valley Cabernet Sauvignon**

Family owned and operated by the Paul Family, Graton Ridge Cellars offers award-winning wines from the Russian River Valley wine growing region. When visiting our tasting room, you will be treated like family and given the opportunity to sample eight or more different wine styles.

Our tasting room is open Friday through Monday from 10:00am to 4:30pm.

Graton Ridge Cellars
www.gratonridge.com
707-823-3040
3561 Gravenstein Hwy North • Sebastopol, CA 95472

Mushroom Shallot Quiche

Crust

    1 9-inch house-made or purchased pie crust

Butter 9 1/2-inch round fluted tart pan with removable bottom. Roll out dough on lightly floured surface to 12-inch round. Transfer to pan, pressing onto bottom and up sides; trim any excess. Chill 1 hour.

Filling

1 1/2 tablespoons unsalted butter
1/3 cup shallots (about 2 medium), chopped
1/2 pound mushrooms, cut into 1/4-inch slices
5 teaspoons fresh thyme, chopped and divided
3/4 cup whipping cream

2 large eggs
Pinch of salt
Pinch of ground black pepper
2 green onions (white and pale green parts only), thinly sliced
2 tablespoons Gruyère cheese, finely grated

Preheat oven to 400 degrees Fahrenheit.

Butter large square of foil and press, butter side down, onto crust. Fill with pie weights or dried beans. Bake 20 minutes. Remove foil and weights. Using fork, pierce bottom of crust all over (about 10 times). Bake until golden, about 10 minutes. Brush lightly with egg white. Cool. Can be baked 6 hours ahead. Let stand at room temperature.

Filling: Melt butter in large nonstick skillet over medium heat. Add shallots; sauté until soft, about 2 minutes. Add mushrooms; sprinkle with salt and pepper. Increase heat to high and sauté until liquid absorbed and mushrooms tender, about 8 minutes. Sprinkle with 2 1/2 teaspoons thyme; cook 1 minute. Transfer mixture to plate; cool mushrooms completely.

Preheat oven to 350 degrees Fahrenheit.

Place cooled crust in pan on baking sheet. Sprinkle with remaining 2 1/2 teaspoons thyme. Drain mushrooms, if needed. Scatter mushrooms over thyme. Whisk cream, eggs, salt, and pepper in medium bowl. Pour egg mixture over mushrooms. Sprinkle with green onions and cheese. Bake quiche until custard is set, about 25 minutes. Cool 15 minutes. Serve warm or at room temperature.

Serves: 6

Suggested Pairing   **2007 Graton Ridge Pinot Noir**

Pomegranate-Grilled Lamb Chops

Marinade

1 3/4 cups fresh pomegranate seeds
4 garlic cloves, crushed
6 black peppercorns, crushed
1/3 cup finely chopped mint
Salt to taste

8 rib lamb chops (3/4 inch thick)
2 tablespoons olive oil
Mint leaves for garnish
2 tablespoons pomegranate seeds for garnish

Combine marinade ingredients in ceramic bowl. Add chops, refrigerate overnight.

Take chops out of marinade and set aside.

Pour marinade into small saucepan and cook for 20 minutes or until reduced to 1/3 cup. Brush chops with marinade and 2 tablespoons olive oil.

Grill about 5 minutes for medium rare, brushing with marinade as needed.

Garnish with mint and pomegranate seeds.

Serves: 4

Suggested Pairing

Gundlach Bundschu Pinot Noir, Estate Vineyard

HARVEST MOON
— ESTATE & WINERY —

Harvest Moon is a small, family-driven winery nestled in the Russian River Valley that focuses primarily on California's own Zinfandel. The proprietors, Bob and Ginny Pitts, have grown grapes since 1977. In 2000, their son Randy assumed the farming responsibilities at the 12-acre family ranch. In 2002 the family received a small production winery permit and now produces 3,000 cases a year of rich, fruit driven Zinfandel and a limited production of handcrafted Pinot Noir and Gewurztraminer.

Harvest Moon Winery
www.harvestmoonwinery.com
707-573-8711
2192 Olivet Road • Santa Rosa, CA 95401

Harvest Moon Brownies

4 ounces Scharffenberger 99% unsweetened chocolate (2 scored sections)
2/3 cup butter
2 cups sugar
4 eggs
1 teaspoon vanilla extract
1 1/3 to 1 1/2 cups unsifted flour (less flour for moister brownies)
1/2 teaspoon salt
1 teaspoon baking powder

Preheat oven to 350 degrees Fahrenheit.

Melt chocolate and butter over low heat in a large, heavy Dutch oven. Remove from heat and mix in sugar with wooden spoon. Crack eggs into the pot, add vanilla, and thoroughly combine with the chocolate (dirtying a whisk is optional).

Mix the flour, salt and baking powder in a bowl. Gently lay this mixture on top of the gooey chocolate mixture. Use a wooden spoon to gently stir everything together just until all the flour is incorporated. Do not over beat.

Pour into greased 9x12-inch (or 8x12-inch) pan. Bake for 25 minutes (check at 20). Brownies are done when toothpick comes out pretty clean. Cool for 10 minutes in pan, then cut into 2-inch squares.

Serves: 24 brownies

Suggested Pairing **Harvest Moon's Estate Late Harvest Zinfandel**

Veteran San Francisco Fireman Cecil De Loach, and wife Christine, purchased their first vineyard in 1970, and began farming grapes and producing wine in the Russian River Valley of Sonoma County. Using grapes from the family vineyards, Hook & Ladder winemaker, Jason De Loach, crafts wines that showcase the quality and character of this region. Three generations of experience and family commitment deliver continuity of style and excellence.

Hook & Ladder Winery
www.hookandladderwinery.com
707-526-2255
2134 Olivet Road • Santa Rosa, CA 95401

Firehouse Frittata

1/2 pound mild Italian
sausage
1/2 pound hot Italian sausage
1 medium-size onion,
chopped
12 eggs
1 cup (1/2 pound) fresh
mushrooms, sliced
2 to 3 medium size zucchini,
thinly sliced
1/4 pound Sonoma jack
cheese, thinly sliced
6 to 8 tomato slices
(3/8 inch-thick)
Salt and freshly ground black
pepper to taste
2 teaspoons chopped fresh
oregano, or 1/2 teaspoon
dried oregano, crumbled
Dry fine sourdough French
bread crumbs
Freshly grated Parmesan
cheese

Preheat oven to 350 degrees Fahrenheit.

Remove the casing from sausages and break up meat into 10- inch ovenproof
skillet. Add onion to skillet and sauté over medium heat until meat and onion
are fully cooked; remove from heat. Beat eggs until light and pour over meat.
Scatter mushrooms and sliced zucchini over egg and top first with layer of
Jack cheese, and then with layer of sliced tomatoes. Sprinkle with salt, pepper,
and oregano. Cover lightly with breadcrumbs and Parmesan cheese. Bake
frittata for 35 to 40 minutes, or until set and lightly browned on top. Remove
from the oven and let stand 10 minutes. Cut into wedges to serve.

Serves: 6 to 8

 **Hook & Ladder Chardonnay,
Station 10 or The Tillerman**

J VINEYARDS & WINERY

Passionate Producers of Luxury Varietal
and Sparkling Wines in
Sonoma County's Russian River Valley

Founded by Judy Jordan in 1986 and expressed through George Bursick's winemaking artistry, J Vineyards & Winery produces site-specific, cool-climate J Vineyards Russian River Valley Pinot Noirs, Chardonnay and Pinot Gris, as well as the highly lauded J Vintage Brut, J Late-Disgorged Vintage Brut, J Brut Rosé Non-Vintage and J Cuvée 20 Brut Non-Vintage. Considered a pioneer in Sonoma County for the enhanced Visitor Center experience, the winery offers award-winning varietal and sparkling wines at its Signature Bar as well as sumptuous food and wine pairings in the Bubble Room paired to perfection by Executive Chef Mark E. Caldwell.

Our varietal and sparkling wines evoke the intriguing character of this unique part of the world--where hip energy meets relaxed Russian River Valley style and contemporary elegance meets classic quality.

J Vineyards & Winery
www.jwine.com
707-431-5400
11447 Old Redwood Highway • Healdsburg, CA 95448

Pan Seared Five Spice Muscovy Duck Breast

Recipe courtesy of Executive Chef Mark E. Caldwell, J Vineyards & Winery

Pinot Noir Reduction

1 cup chicken stock
2 cups veal stock
1 1/2 cups J Vineyards Russian River
   Valley Pinot Noir
2 to 3 Star Anise (whole)
3/4 cup shallots, coarsely chopped

3 sprigs flat-leaf parsley
3 sprigs thyme
2 cloves garlic, crushed
1/2 pound butter, cubed
Salt and pepper to taste

In saucepan over medium high heat reduce chicken and veal stock to 1 cup. In separate saucepan combine wine, star anise, shallots, thyme, parsley and garlic over medium high heat bring to simmer and reduce to 1/4 cup. Strain liquid through chinois (strainer) into reduced stocks. Turn heat to low and whisk in cubed butter. Adjust salt and pepper to desired taste.

Duck Breasts

2 Muscovy duck breasts, boneless (12 to 14 ounces each)
1/4 cup Five Spice powder
Salt and pepper to taste

Preheat oven to 350 degrees Fahrenheit.

Using paper towels pat dry the duck. Use a sharp knife to score the skin on each breast in a crosshatch pattern being careful not to cut into the meat. Season with salt, pepper and five spice powder, and rub spices into breasts, coating the skin well. Let duck sit for 30 minutes.

Place heavy skillet over high heat. No need to add oil or butter as the duck skin will render fat while cooking. When skillet is hot, place duck skin side down and cook for 2 to 3 minutes. Flip duck over and cook another 2 to 3 minutes. Remove from stove, drain fat from pan and place in the oven for 13 to 20 minutes checking the center of the breast with a thermometer to read 135 degrees for medium rare, 140 degrees for medium.

Serve with Oven-Roasted Brussels Sprouts and Wasabi Mashed Potatoes.

 Suggested Pairing **J Vineyards Russian River Valley Pinot Noir**

Kendall-Jackson Wine Center

www.kj.com
707-571-8100
5007 Fulton Road • Fulton, CA 95439

The Kendall-Jackson Wine Center is a wine and food experience not to be missed. Set amid 120 acres of gardens and vines, guests are welcomed at our beautiful château for a variety of tasting, food pairing and Sonoma County winery tour offerings.

Each season offers new educational and sensory experiences in our extensive gardens, demonstration vineyard and tasting room.

Korean Style Kobe Beef Lettuce Wrap

To hold up to our full bodied, complex Cabernet Sauvignon we borrowed the intense flavors of Korean barbeque. Kobe tri-tip is marinated and grilled before being wrapped in a lettuce cup from our garden.

1/2 small onion
8 garlic cloves
1 cup honey
2/3 cup soy sauce
1/4 cup Cabernet Sauvignon
2 tablespoons whiskey
1 teaspoons black pepper, freshly ground
1 teaspoon sesame oil
1/2 tablespoon sesame seeds, toasted
2 1/2 pounds tri-tip, sliced thin against the grain (or Korean-style ribs, ask your butcher to slice these for you)
2 heads red leaf lettuce

Add onion, garlic, honey, soy sauce, wine, whiskey, pepper and sesame oil to blender. Blend on high until smooth. Fold in sesame seeds.

In large bowl, add marinade and tri-tip. Cover and refrigerate for 2 hours.

Preheat grill to high. Remove the tri-tip from marinade and grill for 1 minute per side. Remove from grill and cover tri-tip with aluminum foil. Allow to rest for 5 minutes. Wrap in individual lettuce cups and enjoy.

Serves: 8

Suggested Pairing   **Kendall-Jackson Highland Estates Cabernet Sauvignon**

KENWOOD®

V I N E Y A R D S

Located in the heart of the Sonoma Valley, Kenwood Vineyards is dedicated to producing premium wines truly representative of Sonoma County's world-class vineyards.

Established in 1970, Kenwood sources grapes from dozens of vineyards – many farmed sustainably – in Sonoma County's best appellations, including Russian River Valley, Alexander Valley, Dry Creek Valley and Sonoma Valley. As a result, every Kenwood Vineyards wine – whether Table Wine Series, Sonoma Series, Reserve, Jack London Vineyard or Artist Series – is consistent in quality and consistently delicious.

Jack London
VINEYARD

Kenwood Vineyards

www.kenwoodvineyards.com
707-833-5891
9592 Sonoma Highway • Kenwood, CA 95452

Cantaloupe and Butter Lettuce Salad
with White Balsamic Vinaigrette

Chef Teresa Garcia

> 1 teaspoon fresh thyme
> 2 teaspoons black pepper
> 2 teaspoons whole grain Dijon mustard
> 1 teaspoon Dijon mustard
> 2 teaspoons salt
> 1 teaspoon chopped garlic
> 1/2 cup white balsamic vinegar
> 1 cup extra virgin olive oil

Mix above ingredients except olive oil together in a mixing bowl. Slowly whisk olive oil into the salad dressing. Refrigerate at least 2 hours.

Salad:

> Four heads Bib Butter lettuce
> 1 cantaloupe, cubed
> 1 small red onion, diced
> 8 ounces Prosciutto
> Fresh Parmesan, shaved or grated

Serves 10

Suggested Pairing

**Kenwood Vineyards
Sonoma County Chardonnay**

KORBEL®

CALIFORNIA CHAMPAGNE

Premium California champagne has been Korbel Champagne Cellars' focus since the company was founded in Sonoma County's Russian River Valley in 1882. Its delicate fruit character and fine, persistent bubbles make it the perfect sparkler for every occasion.

Owned and managed by the Heck family since 1954, in addition to award winning California champagne, Korbel also produces one of America's most respected brandies. Since 1889, Korbel Brandy showcases rich character and smooth California style.

Complimentary tours offered daily.

Korbel Champagne Cellars
www.korbel.com
707-824-7000
13250 River Road • Guerneville, CA 95446

Linguine Pasta
Tossed with Meyer Lemon, Pine Nuts, Parsley and Mezzo Secco Cheese

Chef Robin Lehnhoff-McCray

1 pound dry linguine pasta
1 tablespoon fresh Meyer lemon zest
1/4 cup fresh Meyer lemon juice
1 tablespoon fresh garlic, chopped
3/4 cup extra virgin olive oil
Kosher salt and cracked black pepper
   to taste
1 bunch Italian parsley, roughly
   chopped
1/2 cup toasted pine nuts
1 cup shredded Mezzo Secco Cheese
   (dry aged jack)

Cook pasta al dente, rinse and cool. Set aside in large bowl.

In another bowl, whisk together zest, juice, garlic, salt and pepper. Drizzle in olive oil. Pour over pasta along with parsley, pine nuts and cheese. Toss gently with tongs and serve immediately al fresco at room temperature.

Serves: 6

Meyer lemons are smooth skinned and much sweeter and juicier than your average lemon. Originally from China, Meyer lemons grow bountifully throughout northern and southern California.

Mezzo Secco is a jack cheese that is partially dry, slightly softer than a dry jack or reggíano parmesano.

 Suggested Pairing   **Korbel Blanc de Noirs**

Gourmet Foods & Wine from the Russian River Valley

Bounty of Sonoma County Gift Basket

As one of Sonoma County's oldest family-owned farms, we're big on tradition—the kind where everyone stops what they're doing and comes to the table. Let's eat! That means you too—visitors are always welcome at Kozlowski Farms. For more information, visit our website.

Handmade Pies

Kozlowski Farms—Preserving Sonoma's wine country kitchen tradition. At Kozlowski Farms, when we say "It's just like my grandmother used to make," we mean it. All our products began with founder Carmen Kozlowski's legendary recipes, including old fashioned jams, no sugar apple butter, no sugar fruit spreads and homemade pies including Carmen's fabulous Gravenstein apple pie.

Kozlowski Farms
www.kozlowskifarms.com
707-887-1587
5566 Hwy. 116 • Forestville, CA 95436

Key Lime Chipotle Salmon

We believe that the best foods from salad dressings to chipotle grilling sauces begin with the very best ingredients.

4 fresh salmon steaks, 8 to 9 ounces each
1 10-ounce bottle Kozlowski Farms Key Lime & Chipotle Vinaigrette Dressing
2 tablespoons olive oil
1 fresh lime, for garnish
2 tablespoons Kozlowski Farms Orange Marmalade
Fresh dill, for garnish
Salt and pepper, to taste

Wash and dry salmon with paper towels. Salt and pepper the salmon and place in a plastic zip lock bag. Pour dressing over salmon and let marinate for about 2 to 4 hours.

Add olive oil to heavy-duty frying pan and heat over medium heat until pan is hot. Add the salmon steaks and cook for about 5 to 6 minutes turning once, until flesh is opaque and steaks start to brown.

In saucepan bring left over marinade from plastic bag to boil, turn down heat and let simmer for 2 minutes over low heat.

Arrange salmon on warm plates and pour warm dressing over; garnish with sprig of fresh dill and slices of lime.

Serves: 4

Kunde Family Estate is one of the north coast's premier wine estates. Located in the Sonoma Valley, the family's scenic 1,850-acre estate has been managed by five generations since 1904. The winery, built in 1990, produces ultra-premium wines under the guidance of winemaker, Tim Bell. Today, the Kunde family sustainably farms twenty grape varietals on 700-acres of estate vineyards. These ecological efforts were rewarded in 2008 when Kunde won a Governor's Environmental and Economic Leadership Award (GEELA), the State of California's highest environmental honor, and in 2010, was one of the first wineries certified sustainable by the California Sustainable Winegrowing Alliance.

Kunde Family Estate
www.kunde.com
707-833-5501
9825 Sonoma Highway • Kenwood, CA 95452

Bacon Wrapped Filet Mignon

This is a wonderful recipe to use for entertaining. To make it extra special, we use Certified Hereford Beef filets that can be ordered directly from www.BellCreekBeef.com.

4 to 8 ounces filet mignons

4 slices smoked or peppered bacon

8 ounces Cambozola cheese

1/2 pound whole, peeled shallots

2 tablespoons sugar

1/2 cube unsalted butter

1/4 cup olive oil

2 cups Kunde Family Estate Zinfandel Port

6 cups beef stock

Preheat oven to 425 degrees Fahrenheit.

In an oven-proof pan, melt butter with olive oil and shallots. Add sugar and coat shallots well. Place in hot oven tossing twice during cooking time, about 20 minutes or until very brown and caramelized. Remove from oven and deglaze with port. Reduce by half, add stock and bring to a boil. Reduce heat and simmer for 1 hour or until thickened.

Wrap 1 piece of bacon around each filet, securing with butcher twine. Grill to desired doneness. Cut off string. Top with 2 ounces of cheese. Pour heated sauce over cheese to melt. Serve immediately.

Serves: 4

 Suggested Pairing **Kunde Family Estate Cabernet Sauvignon**

Landmark Vineyards

www.landmarkwine.com
707-833-0221
101 Adobe Canyon Road • Kenwood, CA 95452

Landmark Vineyards was established in 1974 and is a family-owned premium winery rich in agricultural roots. Michael Colhoun, great-great-great grandson of John Deere, and his wife, Mary Colhoun, are the proprietors. Nestled at the base of Sugarloaf Mountain in the Sonoma Valley, Landmark epitomizes the rustic grace and harmony that is Sonoma Valley. Landmark is renowned for its outstanding Chardonnay, Pinot Noir and Syrah wines - all have received top reviews from wine critics and can be enjoyed by the flight or by the glass to accompany a picnic in the Courtyard. Every Saturday afternoon visitors get to enjoy live music performed by local artists, and from May through October guests can also enjoy a horse-drawn wagon tour of Landmark's estate vineyard.

Crab and Corn Chowder

Chef Carol Mason*

- 3 pieces Niman Ranch applewood smoked bacon, cut into 1/2 inch pieces
- 1 tablespoon oil
- 1 large leek, white part only, halved and thinly sliced
- 1/3 cup dry white wine
- 2 cups chicken stock
- 2 cups water
- 12 ounces red-skinned potatoes, cut into 1/2 inch cubes
- 2 cups fresh sweet corn
- 1 avocado, peeled, pitted and chopped
- 8 ounces crab meat
- 1/3 cup heavy cream
- 1 to 3 teaspoons lime juice
- Salt and pepper to taste
- Sprigs of cilantro

In a large non-reactive saucepan, warm the oil and add bacon. Cook slowly to render the fat until bacon is crisp. Remove all but 2 tablespoons of the fat. Add the leek and cook, stirring over low heat until softened. Do not brown. Add white wine and reduce over high heat until there are about 2 tablespoons left. Add chicken broth, water and potatoes. Bring to a boil and then reduce heat and simmer uncovered until potatoes are tender, about 10 minutes. Add corn and cook several minutes longer. Just before serving stir in heavy cream and heat thoroughly. Correct seasoning with salt and pepper. Place chowder in serving bowls and garnish each bowl with crab and avocado and a sprig of cilantro.

Serves: 8

* Carol used the Crab and Corn Chowder with the Damaris Chardonnay which was one of those marvelous marriages. The bit of citrus in the Chardonnay worked so well with the unctuousness of the chowder. It's a lovely soup to be used as a first course for a dinner party or equally wonderful for a main course luncheon.

Chef Carol Mason is a graduate of the Cordon Bleu in London, UK and she practiced her culinary skills in Washington DC for many years as a private caterer and educator. Chef Carol has a long time association with Mary Colhoun, Co-Proprietor of Landmark Vineyards and has prepared many memorable lunches and dinners at Landmark.

Suggested Pairing **Landmark Vineyards
Damaris Reserve Chardonnay**

Larson Family Winery
www.larsonfamilywinery.com
707-938-3031
23355 Millerick Road • Sonoma, CA 95476

Larson Family Winery is a working winery, evident from the tanks and wine barrels, but it is so much more. The Larson family has owned this land since the late 1800's, where it was once the bustling port of the old Embarcadero. Years later, it became the biggest rodeo venture in Northern California, run by Tom's Uncle Jack. Today, the family vineyard produces some of the best wines around. We invite you to visit our tasting room to see (and taste) for yourself.

Tuna Tartare with Larson Family Winery Verjus

4 ounces fresh sashimi-grade tuna (skin, bones and sinews removed), diced
2 teaspoons shallots, minced
1 teaspoon chives, minced
1/2 teaspoon orange zest, very finely grated
2 tablespoons extra-virgin olive oil, plus extra for drizzling
1/2 teaspoon verjus
1/4 teaspoon salt
1/4 teaspoon ground white pepper
1 cup baby arugula leaves, stems removed, washed and spun dry
Chopped walnuts, for garnish

In a bowl, combine tuna, shallots, chives, orange zest, 1 1/2 tablespoons of the olive oil, verjus, salt, and pepper.

Arrange arugula on 4 salad plates. Lightly drizzle with some verjus and olive oil. Place 3-inch ring-mold in the center of the arugula and mound the tuna tartare into the mold. Remove mold. Sprinkle each serving with chopped walnuts and drizzle with remaining olive oil.

Serves: 4

Suggested Pairing
Larson Family Winery Pinot Noir

LIMERICK LANE

Limerick Lane Cellars and the Collins Vineyard are set on 30 acres of rolling hillside on the eastern edge of the Russian River Valley AVA, three miles south of the city of Healdsburg. Proprietor and Winegrower Michael Collins and his brother Tom, purchased the property in the late 1970's. Their passion is to create classic, elegant wines reflecting the unique characteristics of the Collins Vineyard. Collins vineyard is largely comprised of old vine blocks of Zinfandel, the oldest planted one hundred years ago. Limerick Lane Cellars is considered one of the premier producers of single vineyard Zinfandels in California. Come for a visit and help us celebrate 100 years of great wine!

Limerick Lane Cellars

www.limericklanewines.com
707-433-9211
1023 Limerick Lane • Healdsburg, CA 95448

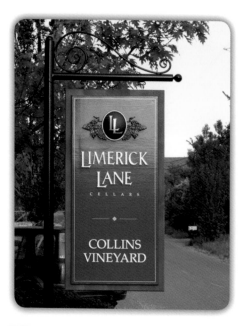

Beef Short Ribs Braised in Red Wine

Chef Peter Leary

Braising is a wonderful cooking method that combines both dry and wet cooking methods. In this recipe, short ribs are browned and then slow cooked in the oven with vegetables, garlic, onions, red wine and fresh herbs until the meat is tender and falling off the bone. The braising liquid is then reduced and used as a finishing sauce. Serve with mashed potatoes or grits and a green vegetable.

3 to 4 pounds beef short ribs
3 tablespoons pure olive oil
Salt and pepper
1 large yellow onion, diced
2 medium carrots, diced
2 stalks celery, diced
2 to 3 cloves garlic, chopped

1 cup red wine, more as needed
1 cup chicken or beef stock, more as needed
4 sprigs fresh thyme
1 teaspoon dried or 1 tablespoon fresh oregano, minced

Preheat oven to 325 degrees Fahrenheit.

Season short ribs with salt and pepper. Heat oil in a Dutch oven pan on medium-high heat. Add short ribs and cook for 10 minutes, turning frequently to brown on all sides. Remove from pan and set aside. Add onions, carrots, celery and garlic to pan and cook until the onions are translucent. Turn heat to high and add half the wine and half the stock to the pan. Cook to reduce by half, stirring and scraping the bottom to remove browned bits from pan. Return short ribs to pan along with thyme and oregano. Add remaining stock and wine to pan. Liquid should come at least 1/3 of the way up side of shanks, but no more than 1/2 way. Cover with tight lid and place on rack in center of oven and cook for 2 hours and 15 minutes.

Remove from oven and return pan to burner. Remove short ribs from pan; they should be tender with the meat falling off the bone. Cook longer if needed. Cover short ribs with foil, put in low oven to keep warm. If there is a lot of fat on top of braising liquid, tilt pan and skim some, but not all, off. You may also remove thyme stems here if you want. Heat liquid on medium high and taste for seasoning, adjust if necessary. It will thicken very nicely over relatively short time. Cook until liquid is at desired consistency. Add stock and/or wine to thin if needed.

Serve on bed of mashed potatoes or grits, spooning sauce over top.

Serves: 6 to 8

 Suggested Pairing   **Collins Vineyard Zinfandel**

Loxton Cellars

www.loxtonwines.com
707-935-7221
11466 Dunbar Road • Glen Ellen, CA 95442

Loxton Cellars strives to be a "reference point" producer of Syrah and Zinfandel. This focus reflects the interests and passion of the owner/winemaker, Chris Loxton, an Australian brought up on a Shiraz vineyard in South Australia, but now living in California where Zinfandel is the adopted grape.

Our wine making philosophy is to carefully manage the vineyard with the grower, pick very ripe fruit and use a relatively noninterventionist method. This involves little or no yeast addition, neither fining or filtering where possible and using only small amounts of newer French oak to help support the fruit, not dominate it.

Roast Lamb
with Olive Crust, Red Bell Pepper Sauce and Basil Oil

3 racks of lamb (1 1/4 to 1 1/2 pounds each), trimmed and frenched
   (cut away from the end of the chop so part of the bone is exposed)
1 1/4 cups olive tapenade
3 cups fresh breadcrumbs made from French bread
Red Bell Pepper Sauce (recipe below)
Basil Oil (recipe below)

Preheat oven to 400 degrees Fahrenheit. Sprinkle lamb with salt and pepper. Spread tapenade over both sides of lamb. Press breadcrumbs onto tapenade, coating completely.

Arrange lamb racks, meat side up, on rimmed baking sheet. Roast until meat thermometer inserted into center of lamb registers 130 degrees Fahrenheit for medium rare, about 35 minutes. Transfer lamb to work surface. Tent with foil; let stand 5 minutes. Cut lamb racks between bones into chops. Spoon Red Bell Pepper Sauce onto plates. Arrange lamb atop sauce. Drizzle some Basil Oil over and serve.

Red Bell Pepper Sauce:
   3 large red bell peppers
   3 tablespoons Sherry vinegar
   1/4 cup plus 2 tablespoons olive oil

Char peppers over gas flame or in broiler until blackened on all sides. Enclose in paper bag; let stand 10 minutes. Peel and seed. Combine peppers and vinegar in processor; puree. With machine running, add oil through feed tube; blend until smooth. Pour into small saucepan. Stir over medium heat just until warm (do not boil). Season with salt and pepper.

Basil Oil:
   1/2 cup (lightly packed) fresh basil leaves
   1/3 cup olive oil

Blanch basil in medium saucepan of boiling water 20 seconds. Drain. Pat basil dry with paper towels. Transfer basil to processor and blend well. With machine running, add oil through feed tube and blend until smooth. Season to taste with salt and pepper.

Serves: 6

Suggested Pairing **Loxton Cellars Syrah**

MARTIN RAY
WINERY

Located in the heart of the Russian River Valley, Martin Ray Winery is one of the oldest winemaking facilities in Sonoma County. Guests enjoy visiting this historic site, picnicking near the vineyards and the ever changing selection of Angeline, Martin Ray and Courtney Benham wines poured in the Tasting Room.

Martin Ray Winery
martinraywinery.com
707-823-2404
2191 Laguna Road • Santa Rosa, CA 95401

Slider Burgers
with Merlot-Caramelized Onions and Blue Cheese

Chef Bruce Riezenman, Park Avenue Catering, Cotati, CA

This recipe is simple, easy and fun to eat. The combination of caramelized onions and blue cheese pairs well with Merlot. Use a good sharp blue like the local Point Reyes Farmstead Blue and excellent quality grass-fed beef.

1 1/2 pounds ground beef, (18 to 20% fat)
1 teaspoon rosemary, chopped
Kosher salt to taste
8 grinds freshly ground black pepper
8 each small rolls (potato rolls or any other style that is soft and small)
1/4 pound blue cheese
1 cup Merlot Caramelized Onions (recipe below)

Preheat oven to 350 degrees Fahrenheit. Preheat a grill to medium-hot.

Form small burger patties approximately 2 1/2 to 3 ounces each. Be careful to press them gently so they remain tender. Sprinkle both sides with salt, ground pepper and rosemary. Rub a little oil on the grill and cook burgers medium-rare.

While sliders are cooking, split buns in half and toast on corner of grill. Place one cooked slider burger on each bun bottom. Top with blue cheese, followed by warm caramelized onions. This ensures the cheese will melt and stay on the burger when you eat it. Cover with bun top.

Merlot Caramelized Onions

This recipe makes more than you need for the burgers. It will keep in the fridge for a couple of weeks. Try it on sandwiches, grilled chicken or steaks.

4 medium red onions,
   peeled and thinly sliced
2 cups Merlot
1/2 cup sugar

2 tablespoons balsamic vinegar
2 bay leaves
Pinch salt
Pinch cayenne

Place all ingredients in heavy-bottomed sauce pot. Turn heat to high, cover tightly and simmer for 15 minutes. Lower heat to medium-high, remove cover and continue cooking for about 45 minutes, stirring occasionally. As liquid starts to thicken, lower heat and stir with wooden spoon until almost evaporated. Allow to cool. Taste and add salt if needed. Store in glass jar in refrigerator. Serve warm or cold.

Serves: 8

Suggested Pairing **Angeline Russian River Valley Merlot**

Merry Edwards Winery

www.merryedwards.com
707-823-7466
2959 Gravenstein Highway North • Sebastopol, CA 95472

One of California's first woman winemakers, Merry Edwards began her career 35 years ago. Her namesake brand was launched in 1997, and 11 years later, she and her husband, Ken Coopersmith, completed their dream winery in Sebastopol. Their growing portfolio of estate vineyards is indicative of their focus on winemaking from the ground up. These properties include Coopersmith, Cresta d'Oro, Flax, Georganne, Meredith Estate and Sanchietti. With exceptional Russian River Valley and Sonoma Coast grapes, Merry Edwards is able to produce acclaimed wines with a sense of place using gentle, traditional winemaking practices.

Merry's wines are available direct from the winery and in fine restaurants throughout the United States. Merry Edwards was voted #1 Most Popular Pinot Noir in the 2009 Wine & Spirits Restaurant Poll for the fourth year out of the past five. Her 2007 Sauvignon Blanc was rated the Top Wine in the 2009 Wine Spectator California Tasting Report for this varietal.

Nestled amid Coopersmith Vineyard, tastings educate visitors about Merry's handcrafted Pinot Noir and Sauvignon Blanc. Merry and her husband, Ken invite you to join them!

Open to the public daily 9:30 am to 4:30 pm

Call us to schedule a private tasting experience Monday through Saturday.

Chicken Valentine

We had several friends over to dinner of Valentine's Day and I was inspired to create this new dish for the occasion.

3 1/2 pounds skinless/boneless chicken breasts
5 medium cloves garlic, mashed
3 tablespoons olive oil
Pinch fresh ground pepper
1 teaspoon tarragon
1/2 teaspoon thyme
1/2 teaspoon marjoram
1/2 cup chicken broth
1/2 cup Merry Edwards Sauvignon Blanc or white wine
1 cup pitted Kalamata olives
3 ounces pancetta, 1/8-inch thick, cut into 1-inch pieces

Preheat oven to 375 degrees Fahrenheit.

Cut chicken into pieces about 3x3 inches. Place pieces in shallow baking dish so that they touch each other and fill the pan. Coat chicken with olive oil, then sprinkle with garlic, pepper and herbs. Turn chicken pieces and rub seasonings onto all surfaces. Allow to marinate for at least 1 hour at room temperature or overnight in refrigerator. Place in oven and roast for 20 minutes. Add pancetta, tucking between pieces of chicken and roast for another 20 minutes. Add chicken broth, wine and olives and continue baking until chicken is tender when pierced with a fork, about 30 minutes more. Serve with fresh asparagus and wild rice.

Serves: 6

 Suggested Pairing **Merry Edwards
Russian River Valley Pinot Noir**

MERRY EDWARDS
2 0 0 8
RUSSIAN RIVER VALLEY
PINOT NOIR

ALCOHOL 14.3% BY VOLUME

Mosaic Restaurant & Wine Lounge
www.mosaiceats.com
707-887-7503
6675 Front Street • Forestville, CA 95436

From the garden to the table, Mosaic's California-Global menu reflects Chef and Owner Tai Olesky's native Sonoma County roots and philosophy of serving local, fresh and seasonal ingredients. Fans are enchanted by this "phenomenal hidden gem" whose "outstanding" locally leaning fare and "excellent selection of boutique bottles" make it one of the best in west Sonoma County. Highly acclaimed in the 2010 Zagat Dining Guide, and a voted for "Best Romantic Dinner" in the Northbay Bohemian Newspaper; join us to experience the best in exquisite cuisine and comfortable atmosphere.

Fennel Pollen Dusted Scallops, Sunchoke Puree and Roasted Tomatoes

5 pounds sunchokes, peeled and coarsely chopped
1/2 bottle white wine
2 cups cream
Juice of 3 lemons
5 pounds pear tomatoes
California extra virgin
   olive oil
Kosher salt
U-8 dry pack scallops
Fennel pollen
Rice oil
Truffle oil
Micro greens for garnish

Sunchoke Puree: Peel and roughly chop chokes. Place in large saucepan and add wine and water until submerged a few inches. Bring to boil, reduce heat and simmer for 2 to 3 hours until cooked through and soft (a little softer than a potato for mashing). Strain liquid, and place cooked sunchokes back into pan. Add cream and lemon juice.   Puree and strain once again. Salt to taste.

Roasted Tomatoes: Preheat oven to 225 degrees Fahrenheit. Quarter tomatoes. Toss with olive oil and salt until thoroughly coated. Place quartered tomatoes on a rack with skin side down. Roast for 2 to 3 hours until chewy and most liquid cooked out.

To Plate: Lightly salt all surface area of scallops. Season both sides liberally with fennel pollen. Heat 2 ounces of rice oil in sauté pan at medium-low heat until oil is moving in pan. Sear scallops 2 to 3 minutes on one side until caramelized golden brown. Flip and finish on other side for about 1 minute. **Do not overcook,** or scallops will become tough and chewy. Place 2 ounces of puree in center of plate and place scallops just off center on top of puree. Lean 3 or 4 pieces of tomato on scallop. Drizzle with truffle oil and top with micro greens for garnish.

Moshin Vineyards Winery
www.moshinvineyards.com
707-433-5499
10295 Westside Road • Healdsburg, CA 95448

Moshin Vineyards is a family-owned and operated solar powered gravity-flow winery located in the heart of the Russian River Valley in California. We handcraft artisan, small-lot wines that exhibit pure and true varietal character. Visit us in our tasting room which is open daily from 11:00am to 4:30pm. Cheers!

Rick Moshin's Famous Smoked Salmon

Smoking the salmon with Pinot Noir-soaked fruitwood chips lends a delicate smokiness to the fish while keeping it moist.

- 1/2 cup of soy sauce
- 1/2 cup water
- 1 tablespoon garlic salt
- 1 tablespoon brown sugar
- 1 tablespoon smoked paprika
- 1 tablespoon black pepper
- 1 tablespoon thyme
- 1 large (3-pound) salmon fillet

Combine first 7 ingredients in zip-top plastic bag. Place salmon fillet in bag and marinate in refrigerator overnight.

Stack charcoal briquettes in barbecue grill and ignite. Meanwhile, soak 1 pound of fruitwood chips, or Pinot Noir grapewood chips if you have them, in 2 to 3 cups of Pinot Noir for 20 minutes. When charcoal is ready, drop chips on glowing coals.

Place salmon on grill away from direct heat and close grill cover. Cook salmon until done and the smoke properly flavors fish, about 30 minutes to 1 hour.

Serves: 4 to 6

Suggested Pairing **Moshin Vineyards Pinot Noir**

Russian River Pinot Noir

MOSHIN
VINEYARDS
2005 Pinot Noir
RUSSIAN RIVER VALLEY
Estate Bottled
ALC. 13% BY VOL.

NICHOLSON RANCH

Nestled in the southern foothills of the Sonoma Valley, the vineyards of Nicholson Ranch are planted in one of the world's most prized grape-growing regions. The Ranch enjoys a combination of soils, sloping hills and climate that is ideal for producing premium grapes for our handcrafted Chardonnay, Pinot Noir, Merlot and Syrah.

Try the recipe on the facing page and then come by for a visit! Our gracious and knowledgeable Ranch Hands will do all they can to make your visit enjoyable.

-Ramona & Deepak

Open Daily:
10am – 6pm

*No Reservations necessary
for groups of 8 or fewer

Nicholson Ranch
www.nicholsonranch.com
707-938-8822
4200 Napa Road • Sonoma, CA 95476

Lobster and Crab Lasagna with Truffle Oil

Chef Tom Romano of Broadway Catering & Events

6 tablespoons butter
6 tablespoons all-purpose flour
4 cups heavy cream
Salt to taste
Freshly ground black pepper to taste
Nutmeg, ground, to taste
1/2 pound fresh baby spinach
8 ounces Parmesan, grated
2 cups ricotta cheese
1 egg
2 teaspoons garlic, chopped
8 ounces mozzarella, grated
3/4 pound lump crabmeat, picked over for cartilage
1 1/2 pounds lobster, cooked and diced
1/2 pound fresh pasta sheets
Truffle oil (optional)

Preheat oven to 350 degrees Fahrenheit.

In medium saucepan over medium heat, melt butter. Stir in flour and cook for 2 minutes. Whisk in cream, 1/2 cup at a time. Season with salt, pepper, and nutmeg. Cook, stirring constantly for 4 to 6 minutes. Remove from heat and stir in spinach and 1/2 of Parmesan. Set aside.

In mixing bowl, combine ricotta cheese, egg, garlic, and mozzarella. Season with salt and pepper. Mix well. Set aside.

Grease an 8x8x2-inch square pan. Spread 1 cup of sauce over bottom of pan. Season crabmeat and lobster with salt and pepper. Sprinkle 1/4 of crabmeat and lobster over sauce. Sprinkle some of remaining Parmesan over crabmeat. Cover with sheet of pasta. Spread 1/4 of cheese filling over pasta. Repeat the layering until all ingredients are used. Top lasagna with remaining cup of sauce. Bake until bubbly and golden, about 45 minutes. Cool for 10 minutes before serving. Drizzle very lightly with truffle oil, if desired.

Serves: 9

Suggested Pairing **Nicholson Ranch Cuvée Natalie Chardonnay**

NIGHTINGALE Breads

Nightingale Breads is all the buzz about town these days. Locals and tourists alike are spreading the word about the outstanding breads being made right in the heart of Forestville. Owner/baker Beth Thorp realized a dream when she opened Nightingale Breads in December of 2008. Many people agree it is the new "jewel" of the county.

The European-style hearth breads are baked fresh in a wood-fired oven with all organic flours and seeds. On the menu is a classic French baguette known as the Forestville French, a Sourdough Batard, a Seeded Multi Grain and a Rosemary Focaccia. There are also some daily selections. Local artisan cheeses, jams, olive oils and vinegars are also for sale to accent the breads.

This is a great stop for picnic supplies on the way to the coast or one of the many wineries in the area. Nightingale Breads invites you to come in and smell the aroma of freshly baked breads. Open Wednesday through Saturday. Call ahead for seasonal hours.

Nightingale Breads
www.nightingalebreads.com
707-887-8887
6665 Front Street, Highway 116 • Forestville, CA 95436

Lemon French Medallions

1 loaf of Forestville French
(about 1 pound) unsliced,
ends trimmed
4 large eggs
1/3 cup sugar
Grated zest of 2 lemons
(preferably Meyer lemons)
1/4 teaspoon salt
1 and 1/2 cups whole milk
1/2 cup half and half
1 teaspoon vanilla
Nutmeg, freshly grated

Slice the baguette into 3/4-inch
slices (approximately 12 slices).

Whisk together eggs, sugar, lemon zest and salt. Then whisk in milk, half and
half and vanilla. Place slices of bread in a shallow dish. Pour egg and milk
mixture over slices. Turn a few times to let slices thoroughly soak up mixture.
Let sit for about 20 minutes. Sprinkle nutmeg over slices.

Note: Allowing bread slices to soak overnight in the refrigerator is another
option to save time.

Preheat oven to 400 degrees Fahrenheit.

Heat a large griddle. Cook slices for about
3 minutes until under sides are golden.
Turn over and brown second sides, about
2 to 3 minutes. Transfer them to greased
baking sheet. Place baking sheet in oven
for about 10 minutes until you see the
little toasts "puff up". Serve hot with real
maple syrup and your favorite fruit and
some bacon or sausage.

Serves: 6

PEDRONCELLI

Sonoma County Wines

Pedroncelli Winery
www.pedroncelli.com
800-836-3894
1220 Canyon Road • Geyserville, CA 95441

Making wine and memories for three generations. The Pedroncelli Winery was established 1927 in the DRY CREEK VALLEY.
Our wines include Cabernet Sauvignon, Chardonnay, Merlot, Pinot Noir, Petite Sirah, Port, Sauvignon Blanc, Sangiovese and Zinfandel.

Stuffed Pork Roast with Zinfandel Glaze

We like this dish with mashed potatoes.

> 3 1/2 to 4 pound boneless pork loin roast with lengthwise pocket
> Cotton string for tying roast
> 1/2 cup dried cherries
> 1/2 cup dried cranberries
> 3 cups Cran-Raspberry juice
> 1 cup almonds, toasted then chopped coarsely
> Zest of 1 lemon
> 2 cups Pedroncelli Zinfandel
> 8 black peppercorns
> 2-inch stick of cinnamon

In a small pan mix cherries, cranberries, juice, nuts, and lemon zest. Heat through and set aside for 2 hours.

Preheat oven to 350 degrees Fahrenheit.

Drain fruit through colander, catching marinade in medium saucepan to use later. Stuff fruit mixture into lengthwise pocket of pork roast and tie with cotton string every 2 inches. Place in roasting pan in center of pre-heated oven. Roast for 30 minutes. Meanwhile, add zinfandel, black peppercorns and cinnamon stick to marinade and heat on medium high until boiling, lower heat and cook for 30 minutes. Remove roast from oven, pour marinade mixture over and return to oven. Baste every 30 minutes, roasting for 25 to 30 minutes per pound. During the last 1/2 hour, baste every 10 minutes. Cool roast, covered with foil, for 15 minutes. Pour off pan juices, straining to catch cinnamon stick and peppercorns. To thicken sauce, pour into saucepan and bring to boil for 10 to 15 minutes. Cut off string and slice roast. Serve with sauce on the side.

Serves: 8

Suggested Pairing

Pedroncelli Dry Creek Valley Mother Clone Zinfandel

RODNEY STRONG
Vineyards

In eight unique vineyards over some 900 acres in Sonoma County, California, Rodney Strong Vineyards produces some of the world's most widely-acclaimed wines. The winery was founded in 1959, by Rodney Strong, one of the pioneers of the modern wine industry in California and Sonoma County. After changes in ownership and direction, Rodney Strong Vineyards was acquired by Klein Family Vintners in 1989, a family-owned farming-based business, and returned to its vineyard roots.

Rodney Strong Vineyards
www.rodneystrong.com
707-431-1533 • 800-678-4763
11455 Old Redwood Highway • Healdsburg, CA 95448

Frisée Salad
with Bacon and Deviled Eggs

Jeff Mall, Zin Restaurant & Wine Bar

Deviled Eggs

6 large eggs
1⁄4 cup mayonnaise
1 1⁄2 pickled jalapeño chiles, minced
2 teaspoons pickled jalapeño juice
   from can

2 teaspoons fresh chives,
   minced, plus more for
   garnish
Kosher salt and freshly
   ground pepper to taste

Frisée Salad

2 heads frisée or curly endive, outer
   leaves discarded
8 slices bacon, cut into small dice
1 shallot, minced
1 teaspoon Dijon mustard

1⁄4 cup sherry vinegar
1⁄4 cup canola oil
Kosher salt and freshly
   ground pepper to taste

Place eggs in deep saucepan and add water to cover. Bring to a boil over high heat, and boil for 1 minute. Remove from heat, cover, and let stand for 10 minutes. Drain water, roll eggs gently around inside pan to crack shells, and place in bowl of ice water for 15 minutes. Peel eggs and cut in half lengthwise. Push yolks through a sieve into small bowl and mix with mayonnaise, jalapeños and juice, chives, salt, and pepper. Spoon yolk mixture into a pastry bag and pipe it into each egg-white half, or spoon it into the halves.

Tear frisée into bite-sized pieces (you should have about 8 cups). In medium skillet, cook bacon over medium-high heat until crisp and browned, 8 to 10 minutes. Remove from heat. Using slotted spoon, transfer bacon to paper

towels and discard all but 2 tablespoons of fat from pan. Add shallot, mustard, and vinegar to pan and whisk to blend. Gradually whisk in oil until emulsified. Season with salt and pepper. Add warm dressing and bacon to frisée and toss.

To serve, divide salad among 4 salad plates. Top each salad with 3 deviled egg halves, garnish with chives, and serve.

Serves: 4 as first course

Suggested Pairing **Rodney Strong Charlotte's Home Sauvignon Blanc**

ROUTE 128
Vineyards & Winery

Pete and Lorna Opatz, with careers spanning over half a century in the wine industry, have combined skills and dreams in their family winery, Route 128 Winery, named for the highway that runs by their home and family vineyard at 1,400 feet in the Yorkville Highlands. In 2003 their small lot wine production began with Viognier, followed in 2004 with Syrah and Zinfandel, for a combined total of 450 cases annually. "We grow it, blend it, bottle it and pop! the cork for you at our Tasting Room in downtown Geyserville, eager to share our hand-made artisan wines with you."

Route 128 Winery
www.route128winery.com
707-696-0004
21079 Geyserville Avenue • Geyserville, CA 95441

Syrah-Marinated Tenderloin with Blueberries

1 3-pound beef tenderloin
1 cup dried blueberries, mashed
2 cups Route 128 Syrah
1/4 cup white grape juice con-
   centrate
3 tablespoons brown sugar
2 tablespoons soy sauce
1 teaspoon coarse ground pepper
1/4 teaspoon salt
3 garlic cloves, minced
Peanut oil, or canola
1 tablespoon all-purpose flour
Thyme sprig (optional)

ROUTE 128

SYRAH

OPATZ FAMILY VINEYARD
Yorkville Highlands

2006
ALC. 14.7% BY VOL.

Trim fat from tenderloin. Combine tenderloin and next 8 ingredients in large zip-top plastic bag, and seal bag. Marinate in refrigerator 24 hours, turning bag occasionally. Remove tenderloin from bag, reserving marinade.

Preheat oven to 500 degrees Fahrenheit.

Place tenderloin on broiler pan coated with peanut oil. Insert meat thermometer into thickest portion of tenderloin. Place in oven; immediately reduce oven temp to 350 degrees; bake 1 hour and 10 minutes or until thermometer registers 145 degrees (medium-rare) to 160 degrees (medium). Let stand 10 minutes.

Whisk flour and 2 tablespoons reserved marinade in a large skillet. Add remaining marinade to skillet, whisking until blended. Bring to boil; cook 8 minutes or until thick, stirring constantly. Serve warm with tenderloin. Garnish with thyme sprigs, if desired.

Serves: 12 (3-ounce serving of beef and about 2 tablespoons sauce)

Suggested Pairing   **Route 128 Winery**
Opatz Family Vineyard Syrah

Russian Hill Estate, a family owned and operated winery, is located in the heart of the Russian River Valley. Using the utmost care from vineyard to bottle, Russian Hill is dedicated to the production of world-class Pinot noir and Syrah. The key philosophy of the winery is to maintain the highest degree of excellence in viticultural and winemaking practices to allow wines to fully express the various vineyards that are their source.

Russian Hill Estate Winery
www.russianhillwinery.com
707-575-9428
4525 Slusser Road • Windsor CA 95492

Lemony Spiced Tandoor Chicken

We enjoy pairing such dishes with our Top Block Syrah where the floral aromas and tones of honeysuckle and jasmine pair well with the rich, exotic spice flavors of Indian cuisine.

6 chicken breasts or 6 game hens (wings and neck removed)

1/4 cup fresh lemon juice, plus lemon wedges for serving

Salt

1 tablespoon plus 1 teaspoon hot paprika

1 cup whole milk yogurt

1/4 cup fresh ginger, coarsely chopped

1 tablespoon garam masala ("warm spice" a blend of cloves, cinnamon, cardamom, nutmeg, mace, cumin and coriander) can be found in the condiment aisle

4 cloves garlic, coarsely chopped

1 tablespoon unsweetened toasted wheat germ

2 tablespoons vegetable oil, plus more for grilling

1 tablespoon extra-virgin olive oil

Freshly ground pepper

1 head of romaine, cut into bite-size pieces

1/2 small red onion, thinly sliced.

Using a sharp knife, make two 1/4 inch deep slashes in each breast (or breast and thighs of game hen). Place chicken on large rimmed baking sheet and drizzle with 2 tablespoons of lemon juice; rub to coat thoroughly. Season chicken with salt and sprinkle with 2 teaspoons of paprika; rub seasonings into slashes. Cover and refrigerate for one hour.

In mini food processor, combine yogurt, ginger, garam masala, garlic, wheat germ, 2 tablespoons of vegetable oil, 1 tablespoon of lemon juice and remaining paprika. Process until smooth. Coat chicken with marinade, cover and refrigerate for 3 hours.

Preheat oven to 400 degrees Fahrenheit.

Heat large grill pan and coat with vegetable oil. Grill chicken over moderately high heat until nicely charred all over. Transfer to large rimmed baking sheet, and roast in oven until juices run clear, approximately 45 minutes. In large bowl combine remaining lemon juice with olive oil and season with salt and pepper. Add romaine and red onion and toss. Mound salad on plates and top with chicken breasts. Serve with lemon wedges.

Serves: 6

 Suggested Pairing **Russian Hill Top Block Syrah**

Russian River Vineyards, in the heart of Sonoma's famed Russian River Valley, is a unique "destination winery" – one of the oldest and most storied in the region. As stewards of this beautiful and historic site, we proudly share our passion for fine wine and our personal commitment to maintain and enhance this extraordinary estate.

Russian River Vineyards
www.russianrivervineyards.com
707-887-3344
5700 Gravenstein Highway North • Forestville, CA 95436

French Onion Soup

2 tablespoons butter
2 tablespoons oil, olive or blend
5 yellow onions, thinly sliced
1 quart beef stock
1 quart chicken stock
1 quart vegetable stock
1 tablespoon thyme
1/2 cup sherry
French baguette, thinly sliced
Parmesan and Gruyere cheese, grated

Sauté onions in butter and oil until golden brown about 15 minutes. Reduce heat to low and cook for 40 minutes; add thyme. Deglaze onions with sherry, add stocks and bring to boil. Add salt and pepper to taste.

Top bread slices with cheeses and toast under broiler.

Ladle soup into bowls and place toasted bread on top. Garnish with thyme.

Serves: 8

Suggested Pairing

**2007 Pinot Noir
RRV Limited**

**2009 Chardonnay
No Oak Russian
River Vineyards**

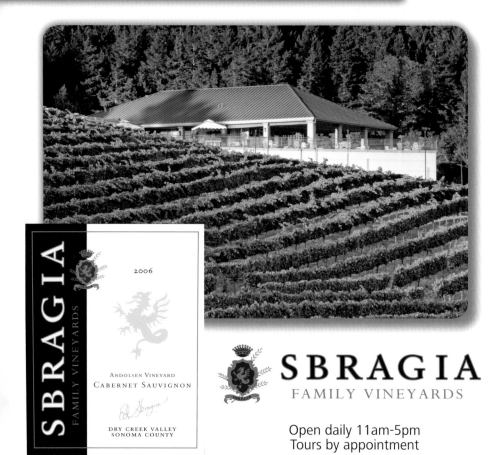

SBRAGIA
FAMILY VINEYARDS

Open daily 11am-5pm
Tours by appointment

Sbragia Family Vineyards prides itself on its single vineyard varietals and small case production. Varieties include Sauvignon Blanc, Chardonnay, Merlot, Zinfandel and Cabernet Sauvignon. Most of the wines are made from vineyards owned by the Sbragia family, but do include select vineyards from Sonoma and Napa Valley as well. Our wines have received many accolades and are considered some of California's best.

Our saying here at the winery is:

"The Only Thing Better Than the View is the Wine"

Sbragia Family Vineyards
www.sbragia.com
707-473-2992
9990 Dry Creek Road • Geyserville, CA 95441

Peppered Crusted Pave of Beef
with Red Wine Reduction
and Blue Cheese Butter
Served on French Baguette

Recipe from Chef Martin Courtman

2x10 ounce New York strip
  steaks, 1-inch thick
1/4 cup fresh ground black
  pepper, coarse

1 ounce olive oil
Salt

First trim all fat and sinew from around the steaks leaving just the meat. Coat entire steak in coarse ground black pepper. Place skillet over high heat and add oil and just as it begins to smoke gently put in the steaks and quickly sear all sides. Once seared steaks should be cooked to rare, about 4 or 5 minutes on each of the 2 largest surfaces. Remove steaks from skillet (save skillet for later use) and let them rest in a warm place for at least 5 minutes before slicing and seasoning with salt and a little more black pepper.

Blue cheese butter
1 cup butter, softened
3/4 cup blue cheese

3/4 cup Italian parsley, chopped
1 tablespoon black pepper
2 teaspoons salt

Place all ingredients in food processor and pulse until well mixed. Remove blue cheese butter and place in a small bowl in refrigerator to chill slightly.

Red wine reduction
2 cups red wine
3 cups beef stock

3 ounces butter, cold, cut into
  1/4-inch pieces
Salt and freshly ground black pepper

Pour off any fat from the skillet steaks were cooked in; then reduce red wine in skillet over medium heat until you have 1/2 cup left. Pour in beef stock and reduce liquid again until you have approximately 1 1/2 cups left. Keeping skillet over the heat; whip butter into the reduction and season with salt and pepper. Strain reduction through a fine mesh and keep warm.

Serve as main entrée or appetizer with each slice of beef placed on piece of sliced French baguette spread with blue cheese butter. The red wine reduction is then drizzled over the beef.

Serves: 8 (as an hors d'oeuvre)

Suggested Pairing   **Sbragia Family Vineyards**
Andolsen Vineyard Cabernet Sauvignon

ST·FRANCIS
WINERY & VINEYARDS

St. Francis Winery & Vineyards, located in the heart of picturesque Sonoma Valley, produces big, bold, full-bodied wines that deliver on flavor. Each wine is crafted from 100% hand-picked Sonoma County fruit and is a direct expression of their winemaking philosophy of "maximum extraction, minimal intervention."

With its stunning mission style Visitors Center located at the foot of majestic Hood Mountain, the Winery offers two tasting bars, lavender dotted gardens and breathtaking panoramic vistas of the Sonoma Valley. It is also one of the only wineries in the area to feature seated wine and food pairings. Each food pairing is artfully created by onsite Executive Chef David Bush and served in a lovely formal dining room adjacent to the main tasting room.

St. Francis Winery & Vineyards
www.stfranciswinery.com
888-675-WINE
100 Pythian Road • Santa Rosa, CA 95409

St. Francis Winery & Vineyards

Pan Roasted Pork Chops
with Tart Dried Cherry
and Balsamic Vinegar Sauce

Executive Chef David Bush of St. Francis Winery

"I like this recipe not only for its simplicity but also because the bold flavors of the balsamic vinegar and tart cherries help to elevate the subtle flavor of the pork."

- 4 pork chops 3/4 to 1 inch thick
- 1/2 cup tart dried cherries
- 3/4 cup balsamic vinegar
- 1/2 cup chicken broth
- 2 tablespoons olive oil
- 1 tablespoon honey
- 2 tablespoons unsalted butter
- Salt and black pepper

Preheat oven to 375 degrees Fahrenheit.

Preheat a heavy bottomed sauté pan over medium high heat.

Season both sides of the chops with salt and black pepper. Add olive oil to preheated sauté pan. Place pork chops in hot olive oil and sear first side until dark and caramelized, flip chops over and place pan in preheated oven. Cook chops for 8 to 10 minutes for medium or until desired doneness. Remove pan from oven and place chops on a serving platter to rest.

Return sauté pan to stove top over medium-high heat. Add chicken broth and dried cherries to pan and reduce by half. Add balsamic vinegar and honey to reduced chicken broth and reduce by half again. Finish sauce by adding butter while sauce is boiling and whisk until butter is fully incorporated.

Spoon sauce and cherries over chops and serve immediately.

Serves: 2 to 4

Suggested Pairing **St. Francis Sonoma County Old Vines Zinfandel**

Suncé Winery, meaning "sun" in Croatian, is located on one of the oldest roads in Sonoma County. Where olive trees once dominated the landscape, old headpruned vines now quietly assert their beauty. Nestled in this serene environment, Suncé Winery provides a tranquil, romantic, yet down-to-earth atmosphere.

The winery, formerly known as One World Winery, was established in 1990. We (proprietors Janae and Frane Franicevic) purchased this new property, which we now call home, during Christmas 1998. We frequently greet visitors in the tasting room, where guests receive a complimentary tasting of four white and five red wines.

Quality is preferred over quantity; each release is limited, sometimes to 200 cases or less.

Photo by Robert Marcus Graphics

Suncé Winery
www.suncewinery.com
707-526-WINE (9463)
1839 Olivet Road • Santa Rosa, CA 95401

Croatian Goulash

1 pound beef, cubed
2 tablespoons hot butter
Flour for dredging
1 teaspoon paprika
1 large onion
1/2 teaspoon pepper
1 teaspoon salt
1 garlic glove, finely minced
3 green bell peppers
1 16-ounce can tomatoes
5 kohlrabi, cubed
1/2 cup water, more if necessary

Roll beef cubes in flour and paprika mixture. Brown meat in two tablespoons of butter, then add garlic, green peppers and onions. Sauté about five minutes. Add canned tomatoes, kohlrabi, salt, pepper and a little water. Simmer slowly until beef is tender. Do not let it cook dry; add water as needed. Cook on low heat for up to six hours or use a crock pot. Serve over cooked noodles or spatzles.

Spatzles

2 large eggs, well beaten
1 pound melted butter
Enough flour to make a thick paste

Combine well beaten eggs and butter. Add enough flour to make thick paste. Using large spoon, rub this mixture through a colander into a pot of boiling water. Stir lightly and boil eleven minutes. Drain. Let cold water run through the spatzles. Sauté in butter for 3 to 5 minutes and serve with goulash.

Serves: 5 to 7

*Suggested
Pairing*

Sunce 2007 Bevill-Mazzocco Vineyard
Cabernet Sauvignon Clone 337

Gold Medal winner from 2010 San Francisco Chronicle

TOAD HOLLOW

VINEYARDS

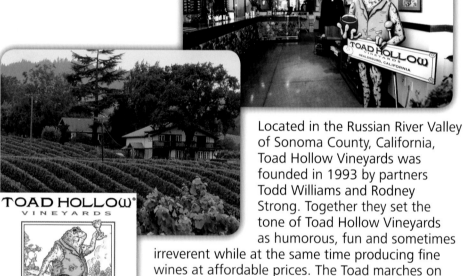

Located in the Russian River Valley of Sonoma County, California, Toad Hollow Vineyards was founded in 1993 by partners Todd Williams and Rodney Strong. Together they set the tone of Toad Hollow Vineyards as humorous, fun and sometimes irreverent while at the same time producing fine wines at affordable prices. The Toad marches on with Frankie Williams, Dr. Toad's wife, carrying the torch that brightly lights the new path for the future of Toad Hollow Vineyards. Toad Hollow was an innovator in the world of unoaked Chardonnay and the first vintage was released in 1993.

Known for the whimsy and charm of their labels, Toad Hollow produces their famous "Francine's Selection, Unoaked Chardonnay" as well as a Russian River Valley single vineyard Pinot Noir and Merlot, a Sonoma County dry rosé of Pinot Noir and a selection of other varietals. Toad Hollow's tasting room is open daily and the entire Toad family looks forward to visitors stopping by to sample the wines, see the labels and hear the story of Toad Hollow Vineyards.

TOAD HOLLOW®
VINEYARDS

FINE WINES AT
REASONABLE PRICES!

Toad Hollow Vineyards

www.toadhollow.com
707-431-8667
409 A Healdsburg Avenue   • Healdsburg, CA 95448

Potato Leek Soup
with White Truffle Oil and Chives

Debbie Rickards (from our tasting room) made this soup for her son Matt every year for his birthday while he was growing up. His favorite birthday dinner was potato soup and hamburgers. The white truffle oil and chives were a later addition to the recipe – more suited for the taste of an adult palate. Enjoy!

1 stick of butter
6 large leeks
5 to 6 shallots, thinly sliced
1 onion, thinly sliced
4 to 5 garlic cloves, minced
2 to 3 large russet potatoes, peeled and sliced
8 to 10 sprigs fresh thyme
4 to 5 sprigs fresh Italian parsley
4 bay leaves
6 to 10 black peppercorns, whole
8 to 10 cups chicken stock (homemade is best)
1 1/2 cups heavy cream
Salt and pepper to taste
1 large bunch chives
White truffle oil (use sparingly)

Wash leeks thoroughly. Trim off and discard dark green ends. Use only white and light green parts and slice thin. Melt butter in large sauce pan. Sauté thinly sliced leeks, onion and shallots over medium heat until they soft and tender. Do not allow to brown - you want this soup to be white. Add minced garlic and continue to sauté about 1 or 2 more minutes.

Tie sprigs of thyme and parsley together in a bunch. Add sliced potatoes, herb bunch, bay leaves and whole peppercorns to pot. Cook for 4 to 6 minutes longer. Add chicken stock and simmer for 30 to 40 minutes until potatoes are soft. Turn off heat and let rest for 20 minutes.

Remove herbs, bay leaves and peppercorns. Puree mixture until smooth. Return to low heat and add heavy cream. Simmer until thickened a bit. Add salt and pepper to taste. Garnish servings with sprinkle of freshly chopped chives and a light drizzle of white truffle oil.

Serves: 8 to 10

Suggested Pairing   **Toad Hollow Vineyards**
Francine's Selection Unoaked Chardonnay

Truett Hurst Winery
www.truetthurst.com
707-433-9545
5610 Dry Creek Road • Healdsburg, CA 95448

Tasting Room Hours:
10:00am-5:00pm

Truett Hurst Winery is nestled in the heart of picturesque Dry Creek Valley. Our commitment to earth-friendly stewardship, handcrafted wines and an unforgettable experience for our guests is paramount and echoes throughout everything we do. It can be seen in our 4 acre organic garden, 15-acre heritage clone vineyard of Zinfandel and Petite Sirah, Grove 47 (our 60-year old olive grove and picnic area), and our newly remodeled tasting room utilizing recycled and sustainable materials. Our wine-making style is big, bold and robust. Aged in French oak, our Zins and Petite have become real crowd pleasers and are a great accompaniment to our weekend live music and BBQ's on the patio.

Wendy's Famous Flourless Chocolate Cake

11 ounces 62% semisweet chocolate or other high quality semisweet
   or bittersweet chocolate, coarsely chopped
7 ounces (two sticks minus 1 tablespoon) unsalted butter
5 large eggs
1 cup granulated sugar

Preheat the oven to 350 degrees Fahrenheit, and position the rack in the center.

Butter a 9x2-inch round cake pan and line the bottom with a round of parchment paper.

Set a large bowl over pan of simmering water to create a double boiler. Put butter and chocolate in bowl to melt, whisking occasionally (chocolate burns easily).

Whisk together eggs and sugar in another bowl. Let butter/chocolate mixture cool a little and then whisk into egg/sugar bowl. Pour batter into prepared pan. Place it in larger baking pan and pour warm water into large pan to reach 1/3 of way up sides of cake pan. Cover both pans tightly with sheet of foil and carefully place in oven. (You can also pour warm water into larger pan after you place it on the oven rack to avoid spillage.)

Bake for 1 hour and 15 minutes, until cake appears to have set and your finger comes away clean when you touch the center. Remove cake from water bath and cool completely. Invert pan onto plate and peel off parchment paper.

Serve in thin slices with unsweetened whipped cream.

You can make and refrigerate this cake a few days before serving.

Serves: 12 to 16

Suggested
Pairing

Red Rooster Zinfandel
and our Dessert Wine
made from Portuguese varietals

Wine Country Waldorf Salad

Chef Robin Lehnhoff-McCray

4 large Gravenstein Apples (Fuji ok)
2 cups red seedless grapes
2 cups large diced celery
2 cups candied almonds (recipe below)
1/2 cup golden raisins
1/2 cup mayonnaise
1/2 cup Greek yogurt (plain)
1 tablespoon orange zest
2 tablespoons orange juice
Mixed baby greens

Dice apples into 1/2-inch chunks and toss with orange juice. Add grapes, celery, walnuts, raisins and toss. In small bowl, combine mayonnaise and yogurt with orange zest and pinch of salt. Pour over apple mixture and toss well. Serve on greens.

Candied Almonds

2 cups raw whole almonds
1 egg white
3/4 cup brown sugar
1 teaspoon cinnamon
1/2 teaspoon kosher salt
1/4 teaspoon cayenne pepper

Preheat oven to 375 degrees Fahrenheit.

In small bowl combine brown sugar and spices and set aside. In another bowl, whisk egg white and then toss in almonds along with sugar mixture and stir until all the nuts are coated. Pour nuts in one layer onto sheet pan covered with parchment paper and bake for 10 to 12 minutes. Cool and use or store immediately

Serves: 8

 Suggested Pairing **Valley of the Moon Pinot Blanc**

WINERY & VINEYARDS

SONOMA VALLEY

Not only are we known for our award winning wines, but also for the Tuscan ambience that is seen in every aspect of Viansa. From the breathtaking panoramic views, the Italian inspired villa and marketplace, alluring weddings and events, to the 90-acre wetlands preserve, Viansa is truly an exceptional winery to visit!

Tasting Room Hours
10:00am - 5:00pm
Open 7 days a Week

Viansa Winery
www.Viansa.com
800-995-4740
25200 Arnold Drive, Sonoma, CA 95476

Viansa Cioppino

4 tablespoons Viansa
  extra-virgin olive oil
1 medium onion,
  chopped
4 to 6 cloves garlic,
  crushed
2 bay leaves
1/2 cup diced celery
1 cup Viansa 2007
  Athena
1 quart homemade
  chicken, fish or
  vegetable stock

2 cups homemade tomato sauce or 2 jars Viansa pasta sauce
1 jar Viansa roasted red pepper tapenade
1/2 cup fresh basil, chopped
1/4 cup fresh Italian parsley
2 to 3 tablespoons fresh lemon juice

Seasoning

2 teaspoons Viansa Italian sea salt
1 tablespoons Viansa Tellicherry
  pepper (Indian black peppercorns)
2 tablespoons fresh oregano, chopped
1 tablespoons fennel seeds
1 tablespoons fresh rosemary,
  chopped

Seafood

1/2 pound medium shrimp
1/2 pound scallops
10 fresh mussels
1 1/2 pounds firm white fish,
  chopped in 1-inch pieces
16 fresh clams or oysters
  (optional)

Add Viansa olive oil to large pan, heat on medium heat. Add onion and garlic, sauté 3 minutes. Add bay leaves, celery and 1/2 of seasoning mix. Sauté 6 to 8 minutes. Add Viansa 2007 Athena, stock, tomato sauce, Viansa tapenade, basil and remaining seasoning. Simmer 12 to 14 minutes. Add lemon juice and then seafood. Cover and cook 7 minutes over medium heat. Remove any mussels or clams that do not open. Ladle Cioppino into bowls. Sprinkle with parsley. Serve with fresh crusty Italian bread.

Serves: 5

Suggested Pairing **Viansa 2007 Athena Dolcetto
or 2009 Pinot Grigio**

VJB Vineyards & Cellars
www.vjbcellars.com
707-833-2300
9077 Sonoma Highway • Kenwood, CA 95452

VJB Vineyards & Cellars produces just 5,000 cases annually which is sold exclusively at our Tasting Room and through our wine club. Our family is dedicated to the meritage of two passions; the making of extraordinary wines and unforgettable memories. We invite you to experience for yourself our handcrafted wines and family charm.

Involtini di Maiale
(Cheese Stuffed Pork Rolls)

1 1/2 pounds pork tenderloin (fillets), thinly sliced
4 ounces smoked mozzarella cheese, thinly sliced
3 ounces anchovies in oil, coarsely chopped
4 tablespoons extra-virgin olive oil
Salt and freshly ground pepper to taste
1 cup chicken broth (stock)
3 parsley sprigs to garnish

Flatten pork tenderloin well with a mallet. Place thin slice of cheese and small amount of anchovy fillet in center of each slice. Roll up each fillet and secure with toothpick.

Heat oil in saucepan over medium high heat. Add pork rolls and brown on all sides. Add salt and pepper to taste. Pour in 1/2 cup of chicken broth, turn the heat down to medium low and cook slowly until all liquid is absorbed and brownness has formed on bottom of saucepan. Remove pork rolls, careful not to let them come apart, and arrange on serving dish. Keep warm. Pour remaining chicken broth into saucepan and bring to boil, scrapping up any browned bits. Simmer for a moment and pour sauce over meat rolls. Serve garnished with parsley.

Serves: 6

Suggested Pairing **Our Award-Winning VJB Estate Sangiovese**

243

Woodenhead

The winemaking at Woodenhead is pure and simple, or if you will, Burgundian done California style. Our wine is handcrafted from a hard labor of love in tune to the natural rhythm of the land, the water, the air and the seasons. Our methods are comprised of using wild and inoculated yeast, malolactic cultures, hand punching, basket pressing, French oak and California fruit! No mechanical pumping is employed. Small and unique lots are what we're after, ultra premium being the goal.

Woodenhead Vintners
www.woodenheadwine.com
707-887-2703
5700 River Road • Santa Rosa, CA 95401

244

Wild Mushroom Puff Pastry

After a day of foraging various species of mushrooms in our Northern California forests, Nikolai and Zina prepare the following savory and delectable one course meal, which satisfies the hunter, the vintner and the gourmand. Be flexible with the ingredients, be creative; you'll have fun altering the cheese, the mushrooms, the spices and the greens.

4 large cups black chanterelle mushrooms (or hedgehogs, golden chanterelles or other wild mushrooms) coarsely chopped
2 large cups Swiss chard leaves, no stalks, coarsely chopped
4 shallots, thinly sliced and divided
1 tablespoon olive oil
1 tablespoon red wine vinegar
1 tablespoon butter

1/4 cup dry red wine
1/4 cup pine nuts
1/8 teaspoon freshly ground nutmeg
1 cup grated St. Jorge Cheese (semi-hard cheddar-like) from Matos Cheese Factory in Santa Rosa (or cheese of your choice)
Salt and pepper to taste
1 pound puff pastry dough

Preheat oven to 425 degrees Fahrenheit.

In large skillet, sauté 2 thinly sliced shallots in olive oil until translucent. Add coarsely chopped Swiss chard leaves. Add red wine vinegar, salt and pepper to taste. When wilted, remove from skillet and place contents into bowl and set aside. In same skillet, sauté remaining 2 sliced shallots in butter until translucent. Add black chanterelle mushrooms to skillet and continue sautéing. Add dry red wine and salt and pepper to taste. Cook until mushrooms are soft. Remove from heat, add mushrooms to Swiss chard mixture and mix to combine. Toast fresh pine nuts in skillet and add to mushroom and Swiss chard mixture. Add freshly ground nutmeg to the filling. Mix all together. Let cool.

Roll out 1 pound puff pastry dough to 12x12-inch shape and place on baking sheet. Use only half of the rolled out dough and then leave 1 inch around the edges. Layer half the cheese, the chard and mushroom filling, and remaining cheese. Brush edges of dough with water and fold over the filling and then bottom edges over top edges to completely seal pastry. Brush top with water wash, and cut slits on top in several places for steam to escape. Bake for 25 to 30 minutes until golden brown. Let cool slightly and serve.

Serves: 4

Suggested Pairing

Woodenhead Russian River Valley Pinot Noir or one of our Zinfandels

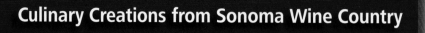
Culinary Creations from Sonoma Wine Country

Index by Category

Culinary Creations from Sonoma Wine Country

Index by Recipe Title

Culinary Creations from Sonoma Wine Country